THE PSYCHIC
DRIVING INSTRUCTOR

THE PSYCHIC DRIVING INSTRUCTOR

AN ORDINARY MAN'S INTRODUCTION TO SPIRITUALISM

DAVID SMITH

authorHOUSE®

AuthorHouse™ UK
1663 Liberty Drive
Bloomington, IN 47403 USA
www.authorhouse.co.uk
Phone: 0800.197.4150

Published by AuthorHouse 04/13/2015

ISBN: 978-1-4969-9282-6 (sc)
ISBN: 978-1-5049-3977-5 (e)

Print information available on the last page.

Any people depicted in stock imagery provided by Thinkstock are models, and such images are being used for illustrative purposes only. Certain stock imagery © Thinkstock.

This book is printed on acid-free paper.

Because of the dynamic nature of the Internet, any web addresses or links contained in this book may have changed since publication and may no longer be valid. The views expressed in this work are solely those of the author and do not necessarily reflect the views of the publisher, and the publisher hereby disclaims any responsibility for them.

For my wife, Ann, who has struggled through this journey with me and still supports me despite the crazy world I have now entered!

And to all the people who have entered my life, because without you I would have no stories to tell.

CONTENTS

PREFACE

I was two thirds into the book and feeling restless one night. I knew that Spirit wanted me to work but I couldn't relax enough to meditate so I opened my laptop and typed the question and immediately started to channel the following passage.

WHAT DO I WRITE ABOUT?

You write about the events that have shaped your life. It seems trivial to think that someone's life could be so interesting but there are reasons why a life should be full of things that you want to say but cannot find the amplifier to say it. It is of no consequence that nobody wants to hear it unless it is the truth spoken from the heart. It should always be the truth otherwise there is no reason to proclaim that you know any differently from anybody else. The reasons you write a book are personal to you but those reasons should never be for money. They should be to involve the world in your belief so that they can benefit from what you know. "How will the book be sold?" I hear you ask. There are ways a book can be sold but it will only be sold if it speaks the truth written from the heart and soul of the writer, otherwise it is just a collection of words on a piece of paper. Like those words, the meaning can be taken literally or can be exposed as a fabrication of an over active imagination. I hope you understand this, as the book you are writing with my help is a study of modern life seen through the eyes of an ordinary man in his quest to re connect with the one true source. I leave you with this thought and wish you well.

My name is Rising Moon, Navajo Chief

WHY AM I WRITING
THIS BOOK?

Good question!

When I was 50 years old I was just a driving instructor from a down to earth working class family with a Wife and two children. I was an ordinary man from Manchester who was brought up on a Cheshire Council estate and liked football, latin and ballroom dancing, playing guitar and a good laugh! I still am an ordinary man but one with a very clear idea of what life is all about and it is not perhaps what you might think it is.

My life changed dramatically and within two years I had the most intense training from the Spirit world that gave me insights into life on the other side, the 2012 Cosmic Moment, the meaning of true unconditional love and how we have lost our connection with spirit and continually defy our intuition in favour of material gain and perceived wealth.

Yet it is our intuition that guides us to make the correct important decisions in our lives.

As a Driving Instructor I had a way of teaching that was slightly different from the usual driving instructor techniques in that I would encourage the pupil to think and make their own decisions. I am not alone in this but many people see my role as one of telling people what to do and how to do it. I always insisted that my role was to make people think and, as I progressed along my "boot camp" Spiritual training, I realized that what I was actually teaching was an intuitive way of working out problems on the road. I used examples of situations far removed from driving to make people think about how these skills could be used in every day life and, as a result, most of my pupils passed their driving test at the first attempt.

I was giving my pupils more than just driving lessons - they were being taught about intuition and how valuable it is. What I was receiving was the insight into intuition in the physical world that would be explained to me in spectacular style when I got the call from the Spirit World.

It is this insight I can now bring to you in simple terms because, after all, I am just an ordinary man!

CHAPTER ONE
MY PSYCHIC JOURNEY

WHO AM I?

I only wish I knew! I thought I had a reasonable idea for the first fifty years but then things changed in the most dramatic way, a change that meant I would never see life (or death) in the same way again. I have read books written by psychics and mediums claiming that they have had psychic, medium-ship or clairvoyant skills since early childhood but I never did. I have had psychic experiences, like a lot of people, but nothing to suggest I would be involved in psychic work in any way. Let me give you an outline of my history pre-psychic days and then you might understand why my current life is quite incredible.

I was born in 1960 at St Mary's Maternity Hospital in Manchester, England. It was the same hospital and year that Mick Hucknall of Simply Red was born (so as time went on I used it as my only claim to fame "I was born in the bed next to Mick Hucknall"!!) The hospital has long gone, replaced by a car park, then modern office buildings so my children were always told I was born in a car park in Manchester!!

My first home was in Longsight, Manchester, a place which would see massive change in my life time. I lived with my Mum and Dad in my Grandma and Grandad's house. My parents couldn't afford to buy a house and there were not enough Council houses to go around. I had an older brother called Derek but he died the year before I was born, aged 4 months from Werdnigg Hoffman disease. I never met him but I was to meet him later in my life in spirit form. I gained a younger brother in 1962.

In 1966, the year England won the World Cup, we moved as part of the Manchester overspill to a council estate in Macclesfield, Cheshire. Manchester Corporation had bought land and built houses in towns in a bid to move people away from the City and solve the crippling housing shortage. We had a back garden instead of a yard. We could play football in the park across the road instead of on a cobbled street. I gained a baby sister when I was eight. We were happy until she became ill with the same disease that took Derek. My Mum and Dad knew she would not live long and she died aged ten months. This was the worst time of my life so far and completely devastated the family but it made me ask a lot of questions.

Up until her death we had gone to Sunday school every week and attended church events with a belief in God but then things changed. The whole family seemed to question how a loving God could take away something as precious as Gillian when she had brought so much love and joy to the family - big questions for an eight year old! We stopped going to church. I went through a very hard time and my parents tried everything to help even though they were suffering their own trauma. Salvation was found in playing football and my brother and I both started playing for Broken Cross under 11s, it was more fun than church (and not as devastating when you lost!) I made the decision at that young age that the only way I would believe in God would be through Gillian and I also boldly claimed to myself that I do not need to go to Church to be a good person.

I went to Kings School, Macclesfield where I spent 5 years in the bottom form ending up with an English O-level and 2 CSEs. I had been helping my Dad at his garage where he was a self employed Motor Mechanic, but with no hope of getting my life on track I went to Macclesfield College to get better qualifications spending three years there and coming out with four more O-levels and two A-Levels, amazing since most of my time was spent drinking in night clubs and playing guitar in a Heavy Metal band!! I should have gone to University but I had had enough of the Education system and wanted to experience work. My Head of Year tried to convince my parents to send me to University, which they would have done willingly as they did with my younger brother later. I had offers from Universities to take me even though I hadn't applied to any!

I started work as a shop assistant at Halfords in Macclesfield, a national motor accessory and bike store. In the first week I was taken aside by the Regional Manager who claimed I was over qualified for the job and promptly offered me a trainee Manager job which took me by surprise. I had a friend who worked for Motorist Discount Centre who were looking for managers and their training was quicker, so I left to join them. They had some very crooked ways and, sure enough, I was sent to work with a manager who was under surveillance for stealing. I was arrested as being under suspicion of being his accomplice and suspended but a week later the charges were dropped and I was free to go back to work. Anybody could see the writing was on the wall so I quickly got a job in a Motor Accessory shop in Leek as a way out but it was never a job I really enjoyed. It only lasted eight months by which time I had been approached by a company that were looking for people to become parts advisors with a BMW Dealership, so I applied and got the job.

By this time I had met my future wife, Ann, and we seemed to hit it off instantly. We used to call ourselves the perfect couple because we seemed to always know what the other was thinking. We got married in 1986 and moved into our first house in a terraced row near the centre of town. Our first child, Caitlin, was born in 1989 and our second,

Mark was born in 1991. Mark became ill as a baby and at nine months old was diagnosed with Neuroblastoma (a cancer of the nervous system). He had lost weight, his lower back and legs had lost their use and he was dying. He had eight months of chemotherapy and recovered and is very much still alive today, as you will find out.

I worked my way up to become the Assistant Parts Manager at the BMW Dealership where I was working and life seemed good.. They were opening another BMW Dealership in Crewe and I was made Parts Manager of this. It was while I was working at Crewe that Mark became ill. As part of a Management shake up I was made redundant just before Christmas and spent five weeks looking for work before a phone call came out of the blue from the owner of the Volvo Dealer in Crewe. After meeting up with them they offered me a job and I became Parts Manager, then Service Manager and things were good again. But I decided to work nearer to home and found a job with the Mercedes-Benz Dealer in Macclesfield, again becoming Parts Manager.

While I had been working in Crewe, I had become frustrated at the harsh environment of the Motor Trade. It was a job for a young man and I wasn't getting any younger.. I felt the pressure of management in the Motor Trade would kill me eventually and I had seen many people seem to age overnight, there was so much back-stabbing going on so for this reason I decided to look for a better career. After looking around for ideas I came across an advert to become a driving instructor. This seemed ideal as training was something I had a desire for and much of the work I was currently doing was training people and bringing them on as well as dealing with work experience, apprentices and hiring. I also loved driving so what better combination could I wish for, so I started training as a driving instructor in my spare time, obviously secretly.

While I was at Mercedes Benz I had gone home one lunch time to be met by two police officers. They asked my name and date of birth and said they had been told to come and see me as the Police had sent a warrant for me to appear at the Magistrates. It was completely out of the blue and the officers assured me it was probably a case of mistaken identity and I would be home later in the afternoon once they had checked it out. They took me to the Police Station while they tried to establish if I was the person the police were looking for but the fax system was down and photographs couldn't be sent so it was decided I would have to go in front of the Magistrates the next day. I spent the night in the cells and, as decided, was taken in a secure van. I was handcuffed for much of the journey and couldn't believe what was happening. Obviously it was a case of mistaken identity but what if this was one of those cases where things go horribly wrong - you read about them all the time. All I knew was that somebody with my name and date of birth was wanted because he didn't turn up for a hearing and now I was being arrested to appear, yet the night before I had been a volunteer for eight year old Mark's cub group while they were doing outdoor activities! While I was in the cell I kept looking up at the window asking "What the hell am I doing here?." I arrived at the Magistrates' court and I had to be handcuffed to a woman police officer to go to the toilet as my cell didn't have one, but that was the least of my problems by now. I was told that if the Magistrates did not have time to see me then I would have to spend another night in the cells, and, as it was Saturday tomorrow, if there were lots of drunks arrested and needed to be seen tomorrow, then I could be detained all weekend. I demanded some action at this point as I had been co-operative so far and this was getting ridiculous now. I went in to see the Magistrates and they had a photograph of the person they needed to see and it wasn't me! They apologized and sent me to the police station to demand they get me on a train home but the duty sergeant refused, so I called the Duty Solicitor and he demanded for it to happen!. They had lost my shoe laces so I came home on the last train bedraggled, tired, without shoelaces in my shoes, to be met and hugged on the platform by Ann, just like a scene from the movies. The next morning I felt very strange and, inevitably, post traumatic stress started to kick in making me feel very depressed as though my life was taking a downward spiral into oblivion. I saw the Doctor who prescribed drugs, took counseling, felt suicidal, was afraid every time the phone rang, couldn't speak to work colleagues and was afraid of my bosses who were actually the best bosses I had ever worked for. I started teaching people to drive in my spare time with the intention of eventually leaving the Motor Trade when I was fully qualified. It seemed the only glimmer of light on the horizon.

Mercedes Benz were closing down a lot of Franchised Dealers to open and own their own and ours was one of them. As part of the change, an Area Parts Manager from our current owners took control of the change, but he and I never saw eye to eye which led to many disagreements. The biggest one was when he told me to sack one of my staff to which I refused to do. He did a good job for me and we would need staff to help with the move - now was not a good time to let people go. It turned out he just didn't like him which I never see as a good reason to deprive someone of their livelihood so the war of attrition got worse until eventually I received a phone call from him in which he said

"You have won this battle, you can keep him, but you will not win the war". He found out about the driving lessons and, sure enough, it was his excuse to put the pressure on. I was called to a meeting with him and my General Manager who had been my ally through all this and I was given an ultimatum – "Quit the Driving School idea and your job is safe" and I was given until the next day to decide. I went into the meeting and told them

"If I said I was going to quit the Driving School I would be lying and I do not want to create a bad situation so it is better if I go now". Both their jaws dropped as they were so convinced I would stay - after all, who would give up a seemingly good Management job with a Mercedes Benz dealership, Mercedes company car and all the status it brings to become a Driving Instructor who hasn't even qualified yet? They offered to get somebody to drive me home but it was a nice day so I said I would walk. After saying goodbye to some of the people there (I had many good colleagues who I had got to know and respect) I walked home and felt a great weight lift off my shoulders.

I built up my business steadily on my trainee license while I trained and, in January 2003, I passed the final exam to fully qualify. I kept building up the business and, while other Driving Instructors were continually moaning about lack of business, I kept busy! I didn't know what it was that I was doing differently but it was working and I just kept on doing it only to discover the secret as time went on.

So that's who I was. Nothing more special than anyone else, some highs, some lows, some weird stuff but all the things that happened would be put into perspective in the most incredible way.

So where was I when things changed?

It was Boxing Day 2010 and I was at a party at my cousin's, but there were a lot of bugs flying around so it seemed everybody in the area was ill! I had a slight bug that wasn't stopping me from working but was making me feel very tired. Ann had flu and was housebound so she couldn't go to the party. By this time she had been battling anxiety and depression for several years that had made our relationship very strained at times. She always told me I should be OK because it wasn't my problem but anybody who has lived with somebody else's depression knows it affects those around just as badly. I had cried myself to sleep several times over the years at the thought that the wonderful woman I married is now just a shell and was incapable of love in the way she used to be. Caitlin should have been coming to the party too but she was too ill and decided not to go at the last minute that caused a heated argument about letting people down. The truth is she was on medication for depression too. So was Mark. He was finding life pretty unbearable at the time and the argument badly affected him so he locked himself in his room and I had to talk him out and persuade him to come to the party and get out of the house for his own sanity, which he did. We went to the party and most of the people there were suffering in one way or another but Mark was the life and soul of the party in his own charismatic way. We had a good time with people we love but came home earlier than we normally would have as I felt tired and I knew there was this festering feeling in our house that wasn't gong to go away.

The next day I went to work and came home only to find Mark had been sent home because of an incident at work which needed to be sorted out. He was in a bad way and Ann knew this, she had had lots of experience at being in a bad way by now so could recognize the signs. Ann herself still had flu and was struggling to cope with low energy and it was her illness that meant I had to cook Christmas Dinner all on my own for seven people on Christmas Day including the washing up where normally we would have shared the workload. Still, another day tomorrow.

Merry Christmas!

TEACHING A MEDIUM

The misconception about driving lessons in the UK is that everybody turns seventeen, passes their driving test, learns to drive the hard way through experience, crashes their car, etc. The reality is that people learn to drive before their driving test otherwise they wouldn't pass! However, like any other business, there are driving instructors who make sure their pupils are ready to drive on their own before their test and can make the transition to independent driving without too much fuss and there are driving instructors who teach pupils the basic skills needed to pass the test but leave them vulnerable to the reality of driving on modern roads. The motive for doing this is usually because they feel that people will not want to pay for lessons - I see it as paying for life training - or it is a way of claiming to get people to test standard quicker so the instructor looks good at the local schools. The pupils are obviously not at test standard and usually fail. However, if they do pass they are now unprepared for the big grown up world of driving but their Driving Instructor becomes a God for getting the pupil through quicker than anybody thought. If they fail, the pupil comes back to them, usually with shattered confidence, so the instructor gains more lessons from them to rebuild it and usually ends up taking them to the test centre three or four times before they pass – extra revenue - so it's win, win for the instructor. I am in the first category and am not prepared to let my pupils be unprepared for anything and this is the reason, I believe, for my success as an instructor and constantly busy diary so far. Many of my pupils are in their twenties and thirties having had driving lessons in the past and had given up for whatever reason.

Sometimes they ran out of money, sometimes patience, sometimes realized it was harder than they thought it would be, sometimes went to University, some who just didn't have the desire to do it. The need to learn to drive catches up with them and they start again with a different desire and motivation. This would lead to a really interesting mix of people who I had the pleasure to teach, amongst them radio presenters, politicians, sports people, people from all around the world.

One such pupil was Carol. She was lovely and was learning to drive for the second time, having given up years before for one reason or another. I could tell she had driven before but, like so many others, lacked confidence and felt she should be better than she was (a human thing!) It was two days after Boxing Day and we had decided to do a two-hour lesson and drive around Gawsworth, a small village near Macclesfield, which was ideal as it was quiet and had just enough challenge to help her with her confidence. We had been driving around Gawsworth for just over an hour and she was getting frustrated with herself but for no good reason. I knew she could do it with a little help from myself and with the chance to build up her confidence. We drove past the lake in front of Gawsworth Hall and, although the temperature was quite warm, there was a mist over the lake as if we were in some setting from the legend of King Arthur! Gawsworth Hall has its own history and legend associated to it with tales of Maggoty Johnson, the last paid Jester in England and stories of a very famous duel to the death in England.

I said to her "The lake looks a bit eerie, doesn't it?"

"Yes" she said, and then asked "Why's that?".

In my voice of authority I said" It will be because of the cold of the air and the heat of the water causing a mist to form" (Physics A Level reduced to wild guessing!). Then I added "or it could be haunted!"

She immediately asked "Do you believe in all that"

"What, ghosts?"

We drove around the bends by the lake and I asked her to pull over at a convenient place (Driving Instructor speak!)

She asked again "Do you believe in it?"

I answered "Well, the ghost of Mary Fitton is supposed to have been seen near Gawsworth Hall because that was her family home when Shakespeare wrote about her in his sonnets, but I don't know anybody who has seen her. I do believe there are spirits and some things we cannot explain."

She then said, "I'm a medium"

WOW! To say that this was exciting was a bit of an understatement because it is a subject I have an interest in and have always thought "Wouldn't it be nice to have that gift" When I think of it now I sound so awestruck!! She continued to tell me how life as a medium was a blessing and a curse. She had access to the spiritual realm but was often found on a night out with friends talking to complete strangers about loved ones and people she could not possibly know about. Her friends just accepted it and would laugh saying "She's talking to spirits again!"

I was fascinated and she started telling me that I had lots of my family around me. I have never in my life doubted it because, as much as I did not confess to having any psychic or spiritual powers, I have felt that people who have passed like Gillian, Grandma, Grandad, etc have never been far away. Partly it was what I believed but mostly it was because of the closeness and complete love that the extended family had always had for each other. Why should this stop after death?

I told her of an incident that happened when I was twenty-one (this will be covered later in the book) and some of the things that I think had happened. She told me these were actual happenings and is proof that my family was around me. I felt really content with that and have always felt comfort knowing that my departed family have always been around me. I then remembered an incident that happened when Mark was ill and thought that now would be the ideal time to ask.

When Mark was having chemotherapy as a baby he would have to undergo an assessment period when he would have to have various scans and tests that were not only unpleasant but troublesome for a one year old. We were at the point in his chemo where these results were critical if he was going to battle his cancer and make a recovery. Living with a child on the edge of survival is something that you learn to live with, but the fear never really goes away. He was in Pendlebury Children Hospital in Salford and had completed the necessary CT scans, bone scans, blood tests and urine tests and was now asleep from the exhaustion. It was early afternoon and the nurse suggested that while he was asleep we should take a break and have some time for ourselves, so we drove to Swinton with the worry that if these results did not show the improvement we were looking for then there was very little chance of him recovering. To give him further treatments unnecessarily would only do more damage than good and we would have to face the reality of losing him. Zombie-like we walked around Swinton shopping centre. We went into Woolworths and Ann wanted to buy something but had no money. I paid with a £10 note and was given back a £5 note and some change. I stuffed it all in my back pocket, something I do not usually do - I usually put notes in my wallet straight away. We went into another shop and I put my hand in my back pocket only to find the £5 note had disappeared! We scrambled the money together but I could not believe our luck could get any worse. It was one of those times when all hope seemed to be deserting us just when we needed it. We re-traced our steps back to Woolworths staring at the ground, desperately hoping to find this £5 note but it was nowhere to be seen. Disconsolate we decided to cut our losses and head back to Mark at the hospital. We walked round a couple of corners in the shopping centre and into a square concrete part far away from the shops and people. Just us. Then, fluttering around in the middle of the square on the floor, a £5 note!! It made us smile but we knew we had bigger problems to confront so we drove back to the hospital.

We arrived back still emotionally drained and walked into the long Victorian corridor of Pendlebury Children Hospital. As we walked along, one of the nurses came running up to us smiling and shouting, "There you are, we've been looking for you, we've got Mark's results back and they're amazing. The lump is much smaller now and he is responding brilliantly to the treatment!" From that moment we never looked back and he made stride after stride. My question to Carol was "Who put the £5 note there?"

Her answer was that spirit will show you signs and distract you sometimes to show you they are there and spirit did indeed show you they were there by distracting you with the £5 note. I was astounded. Here we had a strange moment in our lives perfectly explained by a medium. It made so much sense.

Carol then went on to give me an extraordinary insight into Mark. She said that he was a special spirit, like an angel. He was put on earth for a short time to learn about emotion and the plan was that he should have died from the cancer but decided to stay. He is a special person who has an aura about him and he has a gift for helping and healing. This was his reason for being here and would be his calling in later life. He has work to do before he settles down and might even meet someone whilst he is doing this work. I said he had always had an aura about him when he was young and everybody who met him used to say the same, but he isn't normal, a bit nervy and awkward! She agreed and said he sounded like one of the Crystal children. I could see her look away as if she was listening to somebody then I asked her where she was getting this information from and she said immediately "the spirits are telling me". She said, "as soon as you mentioned him the spirits rushed forward to tell me he is a special child and is a healer. If anybody is suffering he can place his hands over the pain and with concentration and the help of his angels he will give healing. This power may not be there now but it will develop." She said I had psychic tendencies, my family were constantly around me but that Mark was very special.

We had been talking for about twenty minutes and time was ticking on so I suggested we should do some driving, even though I could have stayed all day talking to this remarkable woman. Carol started to drive and she suddenly began to drive really well and enjoy what she was doing, taking great pleasure in the fact that it was going so well. We finished the lesson at her house and I didn't take the full money from her for the lesson on the basis that we had "wasted" time talking about other things than driving. The truth is I should have paid her! I know she gained from my driving instruction but what she had actually done was opened the door to an entirely new world, one which was going to completely change my way of thinking and being.

I went home and Ann was alone in the house. I told her what had happened and we both couldn't quite believe it. How did Carol know about Mark without ever having known him - all she knew was that I had a son who had been ill when he was a baby. We just wanted Mark to be happy, which he wasn't at the moment, but the things she said weren't beyond the realms of possibility, it all seemed to fit Mark's personality. Ann told me to write it down before I forgot it in case it became useful in the future, so I wrote it in an old notebook that contained other diary entries and left it on the arm of the settee to put away later.

I forgot to put it away later, Mark was first up next day to go to work and he picked up the book and read what I had written. I hadn't wanted him to read it because he was in a fragile state of mind and I didn't know what it would do to him. Knowing what I know now, there was a good reason for forgetting to put the book away - there is a greater power at work that does not recognize coincidence, only synchronisity.

The first we realized he had read it was when he suddenly said that night "So I'm an angel am I?" It took us both by surprise and, to be honest, we didn't know what to say. I explained what had happened but none of us knew what would happen next or where it would take us.

I went to work the next day and came home at lunchtime for an hour, only to find Ann sitting at the computer in floods of tears. I asked her what the matter was and she said, "I just typed in Crystal Children and read it and it's Mark – every last detail. Our son is a Crystal child."

We were both totally stunned by what had happened over the last couple of days but what should we do?

We have never been a conventional family in some ways but I suppose this was highlighted by our daughter's assessment of the situation when she said to my wife "Bloody hell, I just thought he was gay not the second coming!." He is neither gay nor the second coming!

Life, like driving, is full of surprises - some days you go off to work and you never know what is round the corner!!

SPIRITUALIST CHURCH

So what next?

To say we had just been hit with a sledgehammer was a bit of an understatement!

At Carol's next driving lesson I asked her about the conversation we had had.

"You knew you could talk to me didn't you?" I asked her

She said "Yes, the Spirits were telling me "Talk to him""

She also told me that she felt she was driving so badly she wanted to just get out of the car and give up but the spirits told her "If you give up then we will stop helping you. Carry on and we will help." She carried on, telling me "that's why my driving suddenly improved, they were helping me"

I told her about the family's reaction and the fact that Mark had not actually fallen apart when he found out about the discussion but had seemed slightly positive about it. She was pleased and said he was welcome to come and talk to her any time he wanted to. I discussed it with him and he seemed quite interested so I gave him her number and left it with him. Surprisingly he rang her up and arranged a reading. The information he received from people he knew in the spirit world was amazing and it also started to answer some of the strange things I had experienced in the past, like my Father in law going round slamming doors in the middle of the night! Over the years I had constantly been woken up suddenly by the sound of a door slamming, believing it was just my imagination and then going back to sleep but, oh no, it was him trying to get my attention and the more I ignored it, the more he slammed them!

As this was Mark's reading and Mark's path, I didn't interfere but Carol suggested going to the Spiritualist Church as there were mediums there every week and it might help to answer some more questions. I suggested this to Mark and he seemed to agree so we decided to go one Tuesday night and see what happened. I have been to see a medium before but always classed it as entertainment, we always seemed to have had a good laugh at some of the messages that came out.

The Church was very different. We were welcomed in and the Chairwoman opened the service. We sang a hymn and it made us smile because, instead of the magnificent organ at the back of the church being played, the Chairwoman reached over and turned on a dodgy cassette player which wobbled its way through the hymn whilst a half dead congregation sang their rendition of a hymn meant to bring joy to the world!! The Chairperson introduced the medium, who gave a philosophy. It wasn't a sermon, more like "A funny thing happened on the way to the church tonight............" and it made us think that spirit was working with us in its own special way. We sang another uplifting hymn and then the medium was introduced as "the bit you've all come to see". This sort of devalued the reason for going, as it seemed to imply that us miserable humans didn't care about the meaning of life, we just wanted a message from the miserable spirits on the other side!

The medium did his thing and seemed to get all the info correct so the congregation went home happy and all for three quid! For all it's failings, this place felt like it was important for the job we had to do, which was to find Mark some focus in his life. That was my focus, I really didn't have any ambition to become part of this phenomenon although I did feel more than happy that I was sensitive to spirit.

I discussed it with Carol and we both felt delighted we had given Mark a direction for his future to which Carol said "meeting you was never about driving lessons, was it? It was about getting in touch with Mark and helping him".

Sometimes you meet people who are only part of your life for a short time but they are there for a reason and will enrich your life if you welcome them in with an open heart. Carol was one such person and, inevitably, having accomplished her mission she gave up driving lessons soon after to concentrate on her own problems in life. But not before she had indirectly introduced us to her Mum, Sarah, who also went to the church. God bless Carol.

Sarah was also psychic and spiritual but not so much as Carol which quietly frustrated her. She introduced herself to us at Church one night as Carol's Mum and immediately took Mark under her wing, as it was clear to her psychic side that he had a lot of bad things in his mind. It was February now but we used to stand outside the church after services and talk for over an hour in the cold, amazed at the things she was saying about spirit. She told us about crystal dowsing with a pendulum and if you had a crystal on a chain and let it hang you could ask simple yes or no questions to spirit and they would move the chain to swing the pendulum in a way that would tell you the answer. Not everybody is successful at this but, of course, both Mark and myself were. Before we knew it we were talking to the dead!! Sarah also said she knew that I would develop quickly but Mark would be better. I doubted that I would develop quickly but she assured me I would and she would be proved right.

The messages from the mediums were also getting clearer. It would be unfair to go into detail about messages Mark received as it is his path and this book is not the place to discuss it. He has his own path, as we all have, and he is still walking it, as we all are. He will be the person to reveal what he has learnt in the future, when he is ready. Needless to say, some of the messages were aimed at us both.

I was told in one message that I was at a fork in the road, one I have been at before but I took the wrong option. She described how spirit would give you these opportunities to follow your path but we are all given freewill. If we choose the wrong option they will always change things around to bring you back to the same choice so you can choose the correct one. This is the fork I have returned to and am now making the correct choice. There is something I can do better than most people but I do not have the confidence to. Other people have the confidence but not the skill. Looking back, I now understand this message but at the time I didn't.

I was told by two different mediums that they could see bright lights in America, like Las Vegas or somewhere similar. I was told by one of them that they could hear the song "Apache" by The Shadows being played.

The most amazing message I was given was from a medium who pointed out Mark and myself. She said we were very close and could almost communicate telepathically with each other. She told me I had been through his struggle and that I was immensely proud of him, almost to the point of bursting! At this point I could have cried because nobody knew the intensity of what we had gone through in a few weeks. Then came the icing on the cake. She said the Angels thank you for bringing him here.

WOW! If ever a struggle felt worth the effort then this has to be it. This isn't a boss giving you a pay rise or getting the man of the match award at football – this came from the ANGELS! I was so emotional and it was like saying that the hard work was worth it as if I had saved his life. How can any father top that?

I was given a very powerful message from one medium. She said she could see lots of gold shimmers around me and waited to see which one came to her first. She was given the name Sam. It was my Grandad. She said he was a quiet man who liked to sit in the background and observe, he also looked like me. I also like to sit and observe and used to do this as a small child. I used to be a daydreamer and needed time to be alone as I was and still am a deep thinker. I could relate to all this perfectly and then she said, "You feel like you have taken the weight of the whole family and helped to pull them through. He has seen your silent tears". It seemed as if I was getting the recognition for being the strong one in the family while they all seemed to be having their individual problems. I was always the one who just kept plodding on and holding things together. I didn't want any credit for it but was just hoping that we could move through it and put it behind us at some stage, but the fact that it was recognized was quite staggering! She continued "You have had this gift since being a small child but are only just developing it. It is as if a bomb has gone off and you are trying to pick up all the pieces and make sense of them but you are now on the right spiritual path. You like to set time limits to achieve things but you cannot do this, you can only do your best, which is what you are doing at the moment. Thumbs up and smiley faces!"

She then brought my Grandma through, saying "You have lots of questions - as one is answered it leads to another question. There is a lot of writing going on because when you are writing I stand beside you reading what you are writing." The writing she referred to was my diary that was now getting fuller and fuller with psychic happenings, such was the frequency of events. My Grandma and Grandad would play a large part in my training.

Although the Spiritual services had given us lots of confirmation, it wasn't helping us to understand how to develop our gifts so I asked the Chairperson how we could join a circle. Mark and I stood there while she told us that she had just started one and it would be unfair to disrupt it to add somebody new. This seemed fair enough but she then turned away from me and started to talk to Mark as if I wasn't there! I couldn't believe it, as it was me who was asking and I was the one who was starting to develop quickly. The next week this happened again, she made a beeline for Mark with lots of information and completely ignored me. I thought it strange but if Mark was benefiting then so be it. It soon became apparent she had a control over the church that she was reluctant to let go. It was my first confrontation with ego in the psychic world and not what I was expecting as I believed these gifts were given by spirit to be used from the heart for the good of the people. She even went to the point of castigating Mark for speaking to other people because she didn't like them. My spirit guides later told me that she did not want me in the circles because she saw me as a threat to her supremacy. However, that was ridiculous as, at that time, I was just a new kid on the block with no idea of medium-ship or any desire to challenge anybody!

As the weeks went on, the mediums came and went, the same people received the same messages from the same spirits, the only thing that changed was the medium delivering the message, so I stopped going. It was now my time to move on and develop somewhere else.

CRYSTAL PENDULUM

It was Mother's Day and we were at a Craft Fair at a local garden centre on a nice Spring day. Inside were many stalls including one belonging to a lady who was selling crystals in all shapes, sizes and colours. There were tumble stones and crystals made up into bracelets and pendants and such like. We had been told about pendant dowsing by Sarah and this seemed the obvious opportunity to buy one and expand the art, as it were. I looked at the pendulums and was drawn to a smoky quartz pendant with nice sides and a long point. I looked at the others but the smoky quartz seemed to attract me more. Anybody who works with crystals will tell you that you do not choose the crystal, it chooses you! If anybody tells you to choose a particular crystal when you are being drawn to another then they are giving you bad advice so, no matter how well meaning that advice may be, always go for the one that you are drawn to because it is the one you need. Call it intuition – remember this word for it is going to be vitally important!

I made sure the pendant gave me the yes/no answers I needed by holding it by the chain and asking for a "yes". Sure enough the chain started making a circular motion, swinging the crystal round in a circle. I asked for a "no" and the crystal swung from side to side. Everybody has a different way of working with crystal pendants so it is important to establish which is yes and which is no before asking questions, otherwise you are going to read the answers incorrectly. When I gave the pendant to the lady to pay for it she started telling me about Smoky Quartz and its properties. Smoky Quartz is excellent for removing negativity from a person or environment, especially where that environment is stressful. I told her I was a driving instructor and she immediately told me that this stone was the perfect choice and I was obviously drawn to it as my job brings with it stress, anxiety and negativity, not only for me but the people I teach. I had simply liked it and not realized that it had chosen me because it was what I needed at that time, so I put it in my pocket and carried on with the day until I got home.

When I got home I pulled it from my pocket and the end half of an inch had broken off! I hadn't had it in a situation where it would have been accidentally damaged so I was naturally puzzled. Any geologists or experts please forgive what I am about to say because I know nothing about the structure of a crystal but I obviously thought it was faulty and must have had a flaw in it! I was disappointed to say the least and explored as much information as I could about crystals from the internet and the limited books I had. I read that if a crystal breaks then it could actually be more powerful because, as opposed to one point, it now has several points and can now transmit more power. I tried asking questions with it and it worked! But it now looked like a dumpy rock on a chain. It also looked darker than I had originally remembered it on the stall. Still feeling it was faulty, I kept it with the thought of taking it back to the stall and changing it but the Craft Fair was only on at bank holidays and special occasions so I would have to wait.

It was a couple of days later and I thought I would try and use the crystal and see if this faulty item would work. To my surprise it did! I asked it several questions including who I was talking to. I was communicating with Matthew, a family member of Ann who had died when he was young over twenty years ago and somebody I had never met. I asked about our family situations and was told we were all receiving help from spirit. I then asked about the crystal

Should I take it back – NO

Should I glue the piece back on – NO

Should I give the broken piece to Ann to help with her negativity – NO

Should I keep the broken piece in the car to absorb negativity – YES

It seemed that, although the crystal was broken, it still worked perfectly. Why shouldn't it? It is a natural material and it's properties are the same no matter what shape it is and the spirit world do not care about the shape or size of it, they are not so bothered about aesthetic or material things, they work on a completely different energy level than us where all that is important is the energy. Remember the word "energy", it is important!

So, the next craft fair came along and, although I had decided to keep the crystal, I took it along anyway to talk to the lady about it. I showed her and she looked stunned. She said she had never seen that before and couldn't understand it but the only reason she could give was that I must have transmitted so much negative energy into it when I first got it that it couldn't absorb it and split with the pressure. It seemed a bit far -fetched but was believable given everything that had been and was going on in my life at the time. She also suggested I cleanse it to filter away any negativity that was still in it. There are several ways to cleanse a crystal depending on it's type and your own personal choice but I held mine under a running cold water tap and asked for the negative energy to be washed away with the water and into the plughole. I imagined the energy disappearing and set my intentions for this to happen. I asked spirit if it was now cleansed and I got the circular "yes" from them. What I did notice over the next few months was that when it needed cleansing, the smoky patterns in the crystal seemed to get larger and darker. Sure enough when I asked spirit they confirmed that it needs cleansing but we were working better together now so I would hold the chain and ask spirit to cleanse it. They would make the crystal swing round and round in decreasing circles until it came to a stop. When I asked if it was now cleansed they would confirm with a "yes" and off we would go again with more questions. Spirit did confirm to me that the reason for the break was excess negative energy but the crystal was a good one for me to use, in fact I still use it today as my favorite dowsing pendulum even though I did buy another "nicer" looking one to replace it!

Bearing in mind this was only fourteen weeks from the first conversation with Carol things had moved fairly quickly already. I was about to take the most intense training course about Spirit gifts, all provided for me by family members in the spirit world!

April 8th

I had heard a clock ticking loudly in our bedroom while I was awake during the night. We didn't have a ticking clock in our bedroom at that time!

I was filling a water bottle ready to take with me to work and had put the bottle down on the kitchen work surface only to be distracted. I came back and the top had gone. I asked Ann and she had not moved it, she didn't even know what I had been doing. I looked everywhere and was about to give up when I noticed it high up on the biscuit tin! Had I put it on the biscuit tin and it had fallen down I could understand it but this had fallen UP! The crystal confirmed it was spirit and by process of elimination I found out it was Ann's Uncle Charlie. He was a joker in real life and was winding me up now!

April 11th

We had a Brabantia set of kitchen tools in the kitchen that was a wedding present in 1986. The scissors have a strong spring in them making them very strong to use but they broke many years ago and, despite many attempts to repair them, we had been using them as they now were. Ann picked them up to use and then yelled "Have you repaired the scissors?" I said "NO" and went to have a look. Sure enough the spring in the scissors had been assembled and the scissors now had the spring action again which had been missing all these years! We were amazed, especially as we had tried many times to repair them and given up because of the strength needed to force the spring parts together.

I was watching football on the tv and asked my pendulum who had repaired the scissors. Again, through process of elimination I found out it was Uncle Charlie. I also asked

Are Manchester City winning? – NO

Are Liverpool winning? – YES

Liverpool were winning three nil!

April 13th

I was woken in the night by 3 loud knocks on the bedroom window. Our window is on the first floor and could only be accessed by ladders!

April 16th

I took some sausages from the freezer in the kitchen and put them in the fridge to defrost overnight in readiness for our Sunday morning fry up, a regular treat in our house!

April 17th

I went to the fridge to get the sausages and they were not there! I asked everybody if they had moved them and, of course, nobody had. I checked the fridge several times for fear of being stupid! I also checked the freezer. I knew exactly the place I had taken them from but they were not in the there either! These were things that could be dismissed as being forgetful but the fact that I could be sure about what I had or hadn't done meant there was no question that other forces were at work.

April 18th

Mark asked "Has anybody moved my headphones?" a simple enough question. Because we were four adults living in a three bedroom semi-detached house that was not big enough meant that Mark's electric piano had to be placed in the hallway. If he was playing his piano you would have to take a detour of the house to get into the kitchen, thank heaven we didn't block any doors up when we first moved in! His headphones were always kept under the piano because he would only ever use them whilst playing – they never moved from there. Yet they had disappeared without trace. We looked all around the house for them but without success.

Ann went to the bathroom and, as she opened the door, the door fell off in her hands! The screws had come clean out of the holes and could not be put back in!

April 20th

Time for some answers! I took out the crystal and started asking questions.

Did spirit knock on my window three times the other night? – YES

Was it for a reason? – YES

Were you trying to make yourself known to me? –YES

Did I put the sausages in the fridge? –YES
Did spirit move them? – YES
Do you know where they are? – YES
Are they in the fridge? – YES

Later I went downstairs to check, opened the fridge and there they were as large as life, staring straight at me, not even hidden!

Did spirit break the bathroom door? – YES
Was it for a reason? – YES
Was it to make yourself known? –YES
Are you going to repair it? – NO
Did you show me the dream of fire and water? – YES
WOW.

On the night of February 28th I was asleep and had the most vivid dream I have ever had. I was standing at the side of water on a quay in a major city looking across the water. On the other side there were also buildings and a bend in the water as if there was a hidden quay behind the buildings. All four of the family were there as if we were on holiday. It wasn't a place I recognized. The reason it was so vivid was that the whole place was on fire! The colours were so vivid – bright red and orange flames on a dark blue water background and the buildings taking a back seat in this amazing explosion of colour. I couldn't make out whether the fire was on our side of the quay or on the other side of the water, it was difficult to make out what was fire and what was reflection but the colours were so vivid. I didn't feel scared but thought it might be best if the four of us got our things together and found another hotel.

On March 10th/11th the Japanese Tsunami hit with the terrible devastation it caused.

March 12th – I was driving home at lunchtime listening to the radio, and there were people describing the scenes around Japan when somebody commented that there was just a scene of water and fire! My ears pricked up and I couldn't wait to get home to check this out. I googled the tsunami and flicked through the images until I came across one that sent me cold. It was the picture I had seen in my dream, the colours were the same, the layout of the quay was the same. The only difference was that the photo was taken from a slightly higher aspect than I saw, it was taken from higher up as opposed to where I had actually been stood on the quayside.

Did spirit show me the tsunami before it happened? – YES

Was the picture I saw from the dream? – YES

Should I have been afraid? – NO

Were you just showing me the power the spirit world has? – YES

Has the spirit world moved Mark's headphones? – YES

Can we have them back?" –YES

Unfortunately the crystal can only answer yes/no questions so the answer to the above was sort of true. What it really meant was "We will give them back when we are happy you have progressed to where we want you to be!"

2nd May

Thinking I had mastery of the crystal pendulum I thought I would find Mark's headphones so I got prepared to go on the biggest wild goose chase ever! I contacted Matthew, who had been very helpful in his training so far and started asking the questions.

Are they in the house? – NO

Are they in the garage? – YES

Are they hidden in the garage – NO

Are they obvious – YES

I searched in the garage but they were nowhere to be seen.

Are they in the garage – NO
Thanks
Are they in the car parked in the carport? –YES
I searched in the car – nothing
Are they in the house – YES
Are they downstairs – NO
Are they upstairs – YES
Are they in the loft – NO
Are they in a bedroom –YES
Are they in Mark's bedroom – NO
Are they in Caitlin's bedroom – YES
She was out at work so I had a quick look – nothing
Are you winding me up – YES
You won't beat me – YES

OK, I get the message. I am dealing with a super intelligence and I am just being a pathetic human being. I would get to know that feeling quite a bit as I walked my path to enlightenment!

I had bought some mixed crystals from the craft fair and was trying to identify them with Matthew's help. It seemed normal to me by now to ask a spirit for help but it was starting to become a bit like a scene from the Addams Family, asking a pendulum "Is this Aventurine?" and getting the answer no or yes and then thanking them for their help! How else do people spend Bank Holidays?

Mark's headphones were to disappear for some time but the challenge from spirit was to find and use my intuition and only then would they be returned.

HEALING

I was quite clear in my reasons for doing what I was doing in these early weeks of this new phenomenon and that was to get as much help as I could for Mark whilst learning about what was happening around me. The Spiritualist Church offered healing services and I suggested to Mark that we should go along and see what happens. I thought it might help him. I had a slight toothache so I told him I was going to go for that anyway and he may as well come along with me (I did think that getting spiritual healing for a toothache was a bit girlie!).

We went in and were met by two healers who told us about healing. We completed the necessary cards. I was immediately told to see the dentist about my tooth (that cover was blown straight away!). I was told, however, that I could benefit from healing.

I was astounded when one of them turned to me and said "How long has your wife been depressed?" I was staggered! Ann had not broadcast this fact and I had certainly never mentioned it to anyone, so it was the first Mark knew about it. We discussed it briefly and I was told that the Spirit world was giving her help for it.

We were led away to a place where the chairs were turned round so the healing could take place. My healer told me to close my eyes and think of somewhere nice so I did. She started to heal, moving her hands around and stopping at certain places in my aura. As the healing continued I began to feel the most intense emotion come over me and I felt as if I could burst into tears at any moment. This was a feeling that was like nothing I had ever experienced in my earthly life and, to be honest, I didn't want it to finish.

When it was finished I asked the healer about the emotion and I was assured it was because my loved ones from the spirit world had come close and were helping me.

We reconvened at the back of the church and I pointed out that Mark has excellent musical ability and could play the organ at the front of the church if they wished. It was an old church organ but the organist had passed away and nobody had played it since, in fact it was out of tune and needed servicing. There was also a grand piano at the front of the church so Mark was invited to play the piano, and at first refused. He is not a performer and runs away from any limelight. Eventually he was persuaded to play and what he played was the most beautiful music, melodic and rambling but none of it familiar (we have heard most of what he plays at home but this was completely different) We all stood in awe, in fact some other people had arrived for the evening circle and they listened too. At the end he was congratulated and one healer said "This church looks empty but I can assure you every seat was full listening to that wonderful music."

As we walked back to the car I asked him "Where did that music come from?" and he answered "I don't know, it just came."

Crystals had an attraction for me at this early time in my path and I would read about their healing properties and which part of the body they would be in tune with. It all seemed a bit wacky that a crystal could cure illness but the idea of everything having a vibration seemed plausible enough, so if that vibration was in tune with the vibration of a part of the human body then that should help to re-align the energies around that area, right?

RIGHT!

A shop had opened called A Little Light and Ann had seen an editorial in the local newspaper with Sue, the owner, stating that the shop had been opened as a meeting place for like minded people to come and talk. She was an angel healer and had been instructed by the Angels that this was the thing that needed to be done. I am grateful they did because this shop was to become a second home for me and several other souls not sure of what was happening! The first time I went in was with Ann and I must have come across as a confused and bewildered man because I had all these experiences being thrown at me and not a clue what to do! What she did pick up immediately was that I was drawn to crystals and that seemed to be something I was destined to explore. She picked up an Angelite tumble stone and put it in my hand and asked "What do you feel?". As I held it I felt a vibration start to pulse in my hand and I knew there was something happening. She said that Angelite is the stone that opens up your connection to the Angels and to hold it and use it whenever I needed the Angels to help and, like everything else I had discovered, it seemed to fit!

So, armed with my new best friend, I set about healing the world! If I heard of somebody who needed healing I would ask my spirit friends, with the help of my crystal pendulum, which stone or crystal would help and put it in my right hand. I had a bowl of various crystals and would let my pendulum hover over the crystals until it would tell me "Yes" over the one to be used. I would put the Angelite in my left hand then close my eyes and pray to the Angels to put healing energy into this stone so it may help the intended patient. I would feel both stones vibrate and this seemed to confirm the job was done, so off they went to the people who had requested them.

We had gone to the mediumship service one Tuesday in May and I wasn't feeling at all well. I felt really down and not in the mood for anything so I asked spirit to leave me alone and give messages to everyone else instead. I was surprised when the medium came to me and I immediately thought "Oh no, now I've got to concentrate!"

He looked slightly confused as if he didn't know where to start or what to say, as if he knew he was with me but did not know why. He said "You're pretty down at the moment but the message I am getting is Physician heal thyself". Now I took that on the night to mean stop feeling sorry for yourself and get on with it but I was to find out in the next couple of weeks exactly what it meant.

The next day I felt ill with a nasal infection and I asked spirit for a crystal. Aventurine was chosen and it cleared up quickly!

The day after that I had a banging headache and asked spirit for a crystal. Blue agate was chosen and the headache went within half an hour!

Later on I had a really blocked nose and, again, I asked spirit and was guided to Aquamarine. My nose unblocked within half an hour!

On the Saturday of the same week we went to see my cousin and her family. After a lovely day, I was driving home and I suddenly felt very ill and tired but thought a good night's sleep was all I needed. However, the next day it got worse and turned into flu. I went to play football despite feeling rough (a regular Sunday night treat and any man knows football is more important than life or death!) and hurt my shoulder. I was in a really sorry state. I had previously bought a crystal necklace off Ebay because I thought it looked nice but I wore it today and it would turn out to be a healing necklace for me (there are no coincidences in the spirit world, I bought it for a reason which was now becoming obvious!). So I went to bed on Sunday night with flu and a bad shoulder from football, dreading the morning and not being able to work. However, I woke up the next day and felt ok for work, and as the day went on I felt stronger and stronger and by Monday evening I was cured. I thought this must have been a mild case of flu but my spirit friends assured me that this was indeed full strength flu stating "we have given you this to show you the power of our healing!"

Whilst I had been feeling ill on Sunday, I also prepared crystals for the following people :-

My Dad had been suffering with his legs and back and was not able to walk very far without pain and having to shuffle his feet. So he was the lucky recipient of a tourmaline, fully charged and ready to go! After a few days I asked him how he was getting on and his answer surprised me. He said that when the stone was in his pocket he still had back pain but when he held it in his hand the pain disappeared! My Mum chipped in and said he had walked to the shop and was actually walking quite briskly and picking his feet up off the floor!

My Mum had a Black onyx for her eyes which were giving her awful problems as her eyesight was starting to fade. She told me that she was sitting on the settee watching television and had a thumping headache. She then felt as if somebody was pressing hard on the back of her head and the pain suddenly disappeared!

My Sister in law had fallen down the stairs and hurt her back really badly, so much so she could hardly walk and couldn't work. Under pressure from her employers to get back to work and, after several visits to the doctor, she was at her wits end so I prepared an Agate for Ann to take to her and thought nothing of it until a few days later. She had gone to bed, the only place she could get comfort, and whilst there she felt the bed move as if somebody had just got off it and the springs moved. She felt the most comforting peace while she was in bed and within a couple of days she was back at work! She smiled at the thought of what she might tell her employers when they ask "What treatment have you had while you have been ill?".

Her husband had suffered from Ankylosing Spondylitis for many years, which is an unpleasant disease leaving the sufferer in pain and discomfort. So he had a stone too. He woke up and stopped taking his medication such was the relief he now had. He had been on this medication for his whole illness and could not suffer the pain without it. He also began fishing again and started a new spiritual journey of his own.

The healing was not only confined to people during this mad two weeks, though. During this time the garden fountain was shooting water three inches higher than normal, the battery powered light under the stairs was brighter than a mains lamp, a damaged blind in the conservatory had been repaired and a dripping tap had been fixed! Ann's car had been knocking at the back underneath and this was mysteriously cured!

When spirit takes control of the training they really work you hard, as these two weeks proved, and there is never a dull moment! But they do know what you can take and when to leave you to ponder, which is what they did for a couple of weeks after. Just enough time to get my breath back.

There are varying opinions of where one should place a stone or crystal whilst healing is taking place. The general consensus seemed to be that gentlemen would place them in their socks and ladies would place them in their bras! The stories of ladies who lost their stones whilst trying on clothes in local boutiques is quite heart warming in itself and paints a picture best viewed in a sit com but, if nothing else, this kind of healing did put a smile on people's faces!

There was one entry in my diary that did perturb me:
"Put Amethyst under Ann's pillow for her hair
Put amethyst under my pillow for my hair restoral"
I still have a bald patch!!!

MEDITATION

As I have written, the first experience of healing was very powerful and took me to a place of great peace and tranquility, a place I wanted to go back to and, through meditation, I would do.

The word "meditation" conjures up all sorts of ideas of strange people crossing their legs and humming in a world of their own, detached from reality in some sort of self indulgent way, or at least that is what I and most of the people I knew felt. Even worse was seeing sandal shod, kaftan-wearing adults hugging trees and dancing around the woods! But, as I began this incredible journey, I started to realize that each person's feelings of "at one" with nature and the universe is a very different experience, as is every person's feelings about meditation.

As I see it, meditation is the art of closing down the mind structure in order to get to the inner self. How you do it is very personal but, until you feel it, it is a place that cannot be explained. The bizarre thing is that we all do it sometimes without realizing it and would never even consider that we have had a "moment's meditation". Losing yourself in a relaxing bath, a welcome cup of tea, a daydream on the bus, we are all guilty of it without realizing it has a name. And it is while we have these moments that we sometimes come up with the most inspiring thoughts, even solutions to problems we have been troubling over for a while. It is no wonder that generations of people were brought up believing that the answer to all problems was to put the kettle on and make a cup of tea! I must admit I do love a cup of tea and any excuse to put the kettle on is fine by me!

I started meditating with the help of books and by word of mouth in what seemed, at times, to be a strange way of relaxing and it was not easy to still the mind of thoughts. As humans we fill our brains with trivia and try to put all this information into an order to make sense of it all. In the end we just have a lot of random information in no particular order, burdening our lives with stress and worry over trivialities when the really important issues are left dormant most of our lives. I'm sure the spirit world despairs when they look at us running around in our little circles! I am not going to give advice on how to meditate because it is a personal thing but I found music a great focus. I could lose myself in the sounds and, before long, I would feel my body grow lighter and my mind would wander into a world I felt happy and relaxed in. This then allows the inner mind to come forward in all its beauty.

As meditation got easier and I could do it for longer I started to get clearer visions and feelings about what was happening. It was during one such meditation that spirit really touched me for the first time. I was lying on the bed listening to music and a candle was burning in the room. Ann came into the bedroom quietly and, seeing I was in mediation, carefully walked round the bed. Straight out of the blue she leant over and gave me a little kiss on the lips. I could feel the kiss lingering, tingling my lips, such was the place I was in. She quietly left the room and, shortly after, I felt a sudden and overwhelming feeling of emotion, similar to the feeling I had during healing. It was so intense there were tears running down my face and, again, I did not want to leave this peaceful and beautiful feeling.

When I finished the meditation I was so excited to find out what or who had given me such emotion, so my pendulum was brought into action. Again, through process of elimination, I asked questions about who had come to me, starting with the people who had come to me before but it was none of them. I continued with the people that I had not had direct contact with yet and was amazed to find it was my Grandma. She had brought messages to me through mediums but this was the first time I had come across her directly and it explained the feelings of great emotion and "coziness" during the meditation. Hers was the first house I had lived in and she was always a source of love to her family. I didn't know it then but she had come to train me and encourage me, just as she had done when she was alive. This began an exciting time in my development because here was my Grandma once again training me, just like she did when she was alive and I suddenly felt like an eight year old again being *TAUGHT BY MY GRANDMA!!!*

From this point on my mediations got easier and I began to sense more things. I can now reveal that when I asked spirit for help choosing crystals for healing, it was my Grandma that would always give me the correct stone. I would look up what I thought was the correct crystal for the job then ask my Grandma's advice and she would either confirm or offer a better one. When I asked if I should study the books more thoroughly having chosen the wrong crystal I would always be told "I will tell you the correct one, you don't need books". In fact, my book went missing one day just when I needed it, only to re-appear after Grandma had given me the correct crystal!

My mediations were now producing feelings of somebody touching my face and hair, a sense of pulsing through my calf muscles, pins and needles through my hands, as well as other sensations. I was beginning to see spirit, lights and shapes on the walls and ceilings, faces in the wall, a couple of arms, and many pairs of hands palmed together. Although I could experience some of these things at that moment, these gifts would disappear again as this was a time of training and spirit was giving me lots of things to consider by showing them to me, creating sounds for me, or getting me to feel the energy, then once these gifts had been recognized and understood a little, they would be taken away and the next stage of training would begin.

During meditation I started to become aware of a feeling that somebody was drawing close to me, the more meditations I did the stronger the feeling would become. I came to recognize the presence by a tingling in my right hand and a feeling that I was being guided by spirit. During one meditation, I saw the shape of a small person in my bedroom. Of all the spirits I had seen, this was the most physical looking but, despite this, I could not recognize who it was due to the fact that the white shrouded figure was void of any detail on the clothes or the face. It actually turned out to be my first spirit guide, a fourteen year old Native American girl which would explain the small size, but she would appear to me once, as clearly as looking at a photograph, like a young Disney Pocahontas! She would bring in new skills and experiences including medium ship, which I was quite excited about having always been in awe of mediums. The way my medium ship started was quite unexpected and again driven by my family in the spirit world, but to understand it more it is better to understand the importance of Gillian in my life.

GILLIAN

As I have mentioned before, Gillian was born at home when I was seven years old and she was a healthy bouncing baby. Unfortunately, my mother recognized something was wrong from her experiences with my older brother Derek, and Gillian was diagnosed with the same muscle wasting disease that had claimed him. At eight years old it was difficult to know what was going on except that Gillian and my parents would go to a specialist hospital in Newcastle-Upon-Tyne and stay away for a few days leaving my brother and I to stay with our Auntie and her family. She had four children and our families had been and still are very close so it was like a holiday for us, although at the time we never fully realized the strain that everybody was feeling. When a situation like this arises life just takes a course that is normal for that time but is not normal for most people.

More than once I would be sent to the phone box just down the road to call the doctor because Gillian was ill and needed immediate attention. Home phones were rare at the time so when the next door neighbour had a phone it saved a lot of running down the street. We just had to give her the money for the call. It was the done thing in those days!

We had a family holiday in a caravan in Rhyl and, on the first day, Gillian became ill. My Dad had been told by our GP what to do in such circumstances and this was to get her to hospital immediately and into an oxygen tent. So we packed up quickly and went to a nearby cottage hospital. They didn't recognize the seriousness of the situation and, after a lot of heated discussion we were sent away. We drove all the way home, seventy five miles or so, and straight to our own hospital where she recovered after being put immediately into an oxygen tent. It is very easy to watch television dramas set in the 1960's as quaint and simpler but perhaps when your daughter or sister is desperately ill then things are not so rosy!

My Dad was a keen photographer and my Mum and Dad would arrange photo sessions with Gillian, my younger brother and I, and dressed us up in our Sunday School Best despite our protestations. The photos still haunt me today – what were we wearing? I realize now that they knew Gillian would not be with us forever and would leave sooner rather than later, so any time with her was precious. I remember coming home from school one day, not long after my eighth birthday, and finding Aunts and Uncles in the house and the curtains drawn. We all said hello and smiled then my Dad took me upstairs to my bedroom. We sat on the edge of the bed then he said "Baby Gillian's died". I cried then just as I am now while I am writing this. My world had just ended.

Gillian was brought home in an open coffin and placed in what was to later become my bedroom. I would go and see her with my parents and I would kiss her forehead, it was like kissing cold porcelain as she silently slept. On the day of her funeral my Dad gave me the card he had written for the flowers from my brother and I. I started to read it. I got half way through then burst into tears. I can't remember what the words said as they were meaningless to me at the time.

As I was slightly older than my brother, I suppose the whole thing seemed to hit me harder than him, I was closer to her than he was only because I could understand her and play with her more. I entered a period of my life I can only describe as dark. I would cry at the school gates every morning, I didn't want to leave my Mum. I questioned. The whole family questioned. We stopped going to church. God had let us down badly. I remember being taken into the Headmaster's office with my Mum to see Mr Swaine. He asked questions about my behaviour and tried to find out the reason for it then he asked "Is it because of Gillian?" I will never forget him asking me this, it was one of those milestones in your life you never forget and I am eternally grateful to him. I can now look back and see that although I had my crisis to get through, it was only adding to the hurt that the people around me were feeling, my Mum, Dad, the extended family, my teachers and friends. To all those people I say, "Please forgive me and I thank you from the bottom of my heart"

Several years later, about thirteen to be precise, we had all been to my cousin's twenty first birthday party and got back very late as was usual for a family do. My brother was home from University for the party so we were all at home again for a short time. I had my own bedroom now. It was the smallest one in the house but, as often happens, the eldest child demands his own space and ends up in the only room available which happens to be the smallest one because it is never big enough to be used for anything! It was also the one where Gillian had been laid out before her funeral but I had been in it for a few years since then and it was my space.

During the night, I was woken up by the blankets being pulled over my head. I was half asleep so gently pulled them back. They were pulled over my head again so again I gently pulled them back, still half asleep but starting to come round. They were pulled for a third time and this time I was annoyed so I grabbed them back angrily! It was at this point my brain woke up in sheer panic at what was happening! My bed was firmly placed with the head against the wall so nobody could stand behind it. The left side of the bed was against the wall so nobody could stand there. The third side had my wardrobe next to it so you could only stand halfway down the bed making it very difficult to pull the covers over my head without leaning on the bed.

"S**t"!

I grabbed the covers tightly, fully awake now, and immediately went into a cold sweat. There are many phrases we use in modern life that have become so overused and out of context we have lost the meaning of them so let me explain cold sweat. A cold sweat is when you are sweating from every pore in your body but it is extremely cold and your sweat is like ice!

Then little footsteps began to run along the bed starting at the foot and running to my face! I could feel the bed push down with every footstep and when they reached my face they ran towards the foot of the bed again. I did the only thing I could do in a state of fear, I shouted for my Mum (I was only twenty at the time!). The problem was that my body was frozen and when I shouted "Mam" nothing came out! As the footsteps got near my face again I shouted again and this time the word came out "MAM". At that point the footsteps stopped immediately and the room fell into a deathly silence. Again the term deathly silence is overused and I cannot describe this sound, there isn't a description I can use. Imagine the whole of sound being sucked out of a room and leaving a vacuum of sound – you can't! Through all the fear of something strange happening I never felt threatened, the fear was more of my logical mind not being able to compute what was happening. I was fully awake and, while I lay frozen in bed, I heard one of the other men in the house get up and go to the toilet for a wee. I know it was a man because of the sound it made from the height it would have come from! Eventually I fell asleep again.

In the morning I woke up with an incredible feeling of joy and happiness. I remembered what had happened and tried to explain it in my mind. I even looked under my bed to see if there was a rogue rat hanging out under there but, to be honest, I didn't care. I went to work on a real high and had a fantastic day. I came home and it was like walking into a black and white movie except I was in colour, such was the feeling of joy!

While we were all sitting in the living room I asked "Did anyone hear anything strange last night?"

Of course the answer was "No" so I told them the story of what happened.

My Dad asked "Are you sure you weren't asleep and dreamt it?" to which I said "One of the men got up just after it and went for a wee"

My brother said "I went for a wee in the night", which gave my story some credibility. The room was quiet while people considered the evidence.

"Do you think it was Gillian?" my Dad asked.

"I don't know"

Then my Mum quietly said "When you were young, one of the games you used to play with Gillian was to pull the covers over her head and it used to make her laugh".

Gillian's illness meant her muscles were wasting away so she couldn't use her arms and legs, and even her neck muscles were not strong enough to hold her head properly. This meant that games were restricted to some very basic ones.

The footsteps? I am sure you have worked this one out - she is ok and she can use her arms and legs again! She had come to see me. I had never doubted she would come back and had never felt she had deserted us but I would never feel completely alone ever again.

After Ann and I got married and were considering children, we thought it only right to check the probability of bringing a child into the world with the same illness so we made an appointment to investigate it. Our path took us to Manchester Royal Infirmary to see a specialist and discuss the situation. I am not good in hospitals so this was quite a brave step for me (I know I'm a wimp!) but I felt good about this even when we went into her room. We discussed it briefly then she produced a six inch thick pile of worn looking notes and put them on her desk. She explained they were Gillian's notes and I immediately felt sick. To say I had been kicked in the solar plexus is an understatement. Every emotion from those dark days around Gillian's illness and death came flooding back and I had to leave the room. The upshot of the meeting was that the odds of anything going wrong were so small it was not worth worrying about, yet the feeling I had was of stepping back in time. it was awful.

When I struggled coming to terms with Gillian's death my Mum had told me "You never get over it but you learn to live with it." She was right but occasionally something reminds you of the darkest times, maybe it's just a way of making you appreciate how far you have come and how much your character has strengthened as a result of this experience.

MEDIUMSHIP

We were still going to the Spiritualist Church for their services and, one week, a medium was scheduled to visit who worked with photographs. This seemed quite exciting but which photograph of which person could I take? Having agonized for some time I decided to bite the bullet and ask my Mum for a photograph of Gillian. I wasn't sure what I was going to uncover and was a little bit worried but if I wanted to speak to anyone in the spirit world then it would be my baby Sister. So, armed with one of Dad's staged photos of Gillian smiling away in a bonnet, we headed for the church.

We were asked to put the photos face down on a table at the front of the church and the medium would be drawn to the one she needed. I was a little apprehensive as I have never seen this done and didn't know what to expect. As the evening began and the medium explained what she was about to do. I felt the pain of all those years ago, similar to when I had been at the hospital. My mind went into a spin and I asked spirit to block any messages for me because I just couldn't handle the emotion and if Gillian was to talk to me then this wasn't the place to do it. I had just refused to speak to my Sister. I felt bad.

I went home distraught at the fact that I had come so close to speaking to Gillian after all these years yet I was the one who had refused the communication.

I asked my crystal if she was there – Yes
Did she want to speak to me – Yes
Will she speak to me again at some time – Yes
I had let her down.

51

Three days later Mark went on a short holiday to Blackpool on his own - he has never been afraid to venture alone. I was feeling down because the house was quieter and I still hadn't come to terms with letting Gillian down. I did a meditation in the evening and saw my Spirit guide. She had been bringing me faces and things for me to look at over the last few days so I asked her if she had brought anybody to see me. She told me she had brought nobody but my family wanted to speak to me. This was new and I was a little bit wary but decided to do it.

First, she brought my Grandma through. She said, "You're doing well. You need to do more healing but I will help you." I asked about my future career to which she replied "Career? What career? Your career will be with spirit and spirit will train you, not books"

Then my Grandad came through. He died just before my A Level exams and I have never forgiven myself for not visiting him just before he died when my parents had asked if I wanted to go. I made the excuse that I was revising for my A levels but if I'd known how ill he was I would have gone to see him. He said "Keep going, Son" He always called his grandson's Son. "Your A levels were more important than visiting me" I told him they weren't but he insisted. I had been forgiven and a huge weight was taken from me.

I asked if Gillian was here and was told "Yes" then there was a long pause before I heard a voice say

"I love you David"

I was dumbstruck but I said "I love you Gillian". For forty years I had been waiting for this moment and it was incredible. I felt so emotional but at the same time I felt I was communicating with an old friend.

"Tuesday night doesn't matter"

"I was only meant to be on earth for a short time"

"I was with Caitlin at her graduation. I'm pleased she has my name" Caitlin's middle name is Gillian after her Aunt in the spirit world. At her graduation her full name was read out and I instantly felt that Gillian was there although I wasn't psychically aware at that time.

I told her that Gillian's illness and death had hurt us all. She said she knew but she was never meant to be here long.

Gillian went away and I was joined by Derek. I was born after he died and he told me "I never had a special purpose on this earth but when I arrived I couldn't handle it and had to go back as soon as I could."

He told me he watches us all and mentioned our brother. He said "He is too fat, he can't stop eating but I will give him some warning signs" I thought this was a strange thing to say but, looking back he did lose weight after this time!

My spirit guide returned and I asked, "Did these conversations really take place?"

I was told "Yes, you need to grow up"

"Are you joking?"

"Yes, I have a sense of humour too"

I was to find out about spirit guides and they can use several ways of making you listen, humour being one of them!

Over the next week I would meditate and my Spirit Guide would bring spirits for me to talk to and ask questions. They were all very obliging and all knew they had been brought to me to help me to train.

I spoke to :-

Ron, a farmer from Wisconsin

Maria, a Polish woman who died in the Concentration Camps and now she now helps survivors come to terms with their guilt at surviving

Kevin, an eight year old boy who died of an illness but didn't know what because "I'm only a boy!"

Alan, who was only young when he was stabbed in a gang fight in the 1950s

Theresa, an eighty four year old biker

Alesha, a seventeen year old who died as a pillion passenger on a motorbike

Eleanor, sixteen when she passed in the 1940s under a bus in the USA

Imelda, who passed from cholera in an air raid shelter during the blitz

Ursula, twenty nine who passed of breast cancer in Sweden

Flossie from Norfolk who moved to America in 1654

John, who passed in Liverpool in the 1960's after being hit on the head in a night club.

Harold, a university lecturer in Norfolk who had a heart attack in a theatre.

Francoise, a nervous clergyman who was hiding children from the Nazis in 1944 before being found and shot.

All these people were brought to me within a week of talking to Gillian for the first time. When spirit know you want to work they are not shy at bringing you homework!

During this "training" period we visited my Mum and Dad for tea, a Sunday tradition for several years now. After tea the table was cleared and the jigsaw revealed for the weekly exercise of staring at it, searching through a few pieces and hoping one would reveal itself to be placed in the jigsaw in the appropriate place! My Dad was sitting on the settee reading and I was sitting on a chair watching. My Spirit guide surprised me by coming to me and saying she had somebody who wants to speak to me. It was Gillian.

"This is nice" she said

"What is" I asked

"Doing a jigsaw together"

"They are always doing jigsaws"

"I know, I keep watching them"

"You should be down here with us"

"No, my place is up here in spirit, I have lots of work to do"

"Do you remember me saying that I would only believe in God if you came back?"

"Yes"

"So does God exist?"

"God is the energy"

I got my answer and now I believe in God again! Except that my view of God is now completely different to the one that I had as an eight year old boy before my Sister was taken away. The God I now believe in is an energy and intelligence so far advanced than us on earth that we can only imagine the vastness of it and is better not to try and explain it. Yet it is an energy that works for us and is us. We are all part of the same energy and it is this energy I now see working every day.

INTUITION

So spirit have trained me in all these skills in less than six months and the one thing they have always insisted is that I use is my intuition! That's easy then, but what is intuition?

In my early days of pendulum swinging I was quite excited that spirit would talk to me and if I gave them a well constructed yes or no question they would give me an honest yes or no answer. But spirit knows when to up the stakes and that is exactly what they did.

The first I knew that spirit were testing me and pushing me was when Mark's headphones disappeared. As you will recall in an earlier section, Matthew had me running all around the house and garage looking for them in vain but it didn't stop me asking. I would suggest a place where the headphones could be and would be given an answer. When I got a "yes" I would check, only to find they were not there. When I asked spirit if they were testing me they would say "yes".

Should I use my intuition? – "Yes"

But how?

They did help me.

I had a little time on my hands one day so I went to the library to see if there were any useful books I could read. If anyone has tried finding books about this kind of thing, you will know that it doesn't fit into any of the orderly categories they have (perhaps that's a message in itself). The psychics I know laugh and tell you that you'll find them in the funny or weird section! As I wandered around the health, self help, or ghost sections that they have decided we belong in, I narrowed the search down to three rows of shelves. As I was scanning the books I heard a crackling in one ear! When I looked at the books, sure enough there were a few psychic books hidden nicely among health and diet books!

I went back to the library looking for Reiki books and, sure enough, as I got near them a buzzing noise sounded in my left ear. As I scanned past, the buzzing went and as I scanned back the buzzing returned like a metal detector! I was interested to read books from mediums about their development so I went to the biography section. I looked for Lisa Williams and received a buzzing as I neared her book. I thought of John Edwards and the same thing happened as I neared his books.

I scanned the spines of the books with my left index finger, as I do, and suddenly my right hand got pins and needles in it. I stopped and checked which book it was- "Turn stress into bliss". I remember thinking it wouldn't be so stressful if you just told me in simple English would it?!

It was a normal Sunday afternoon in May with the family doing their respective Sunday things around the house. We all stopped for a cup of tea and sat in the conservatory when suddenly, in the kitchen, the washing machine stopped mid cycle. It took a while to realize but then Ann asked, "Who turned the washing machine off?" She knew it was a pointless question because we were all in the conservatory but it had to be asked. We went to investigate and the pause button had been pushed in. I also got a tingling in my hands that I knew was spirit. She pushed the button and it re started without any further problems.

We dispersed and I went to clean the inside of my car within an inch of its life! Everything was gleaming inside and you could eat your dinner off the carpets. I took some things inside and went straight back to the car to put the over mats in. I opened the back door and on the floor was a shiny two pound coin. Again I felt a tingling in my hands and could not explain how a two pound coin could magically appear when I knew there was nothing in the car – it was spotless and the coin was brand new and sparkling!

Ann and I discussed these events with great amusement as these things were becoming normal in our house by now. As we looked into the garden two pigeons flew up to the window and landed on the patio just in front of us. They seemed to look at us and walk about as if they wanted to be seen and again I felt the tingling in my hands. This was turning out to be a strange Sunday afternoon!

The pendulum was to provide the answers. Grandad had come to help Grandma by turning off the washer, putting the two pound coin on the mat, and then the pair of them had come to say hello in the guise of pigeons!

I thought it was about time I had a new pendant so I visited A Little Light to buy a new one. I told Sue the reason I was there and proceeded to view the pendants. I was immediately drawn to a point made up of the seven chakra colours. I picked it up and was pleased to start getting the yes no answers I was looking for. Undecided, I continued looking and picking up other pendulums and trying them for their answers. To make sure I was on the right track I had taken my trusty pendulum from home with me to ask if I was choosing the right one. All started OK but, before long, I started to get confusing answers and the spirits seemed to keep changing their minds. This amused Sue greatly. She obviously knew where this was going and wisely let me suffer until the point had been proved. I decided which one to buy and, sure enough, it was the chakra coloured one – the first one I'd tried. Sue laughed and said, "There you are, they are telling you to use your intuition and that was obviously the one you wanted because it was the first one you were drawn to!" Lesson learnt, I put my tail between my legs and sloped off out of the shop like an embarrassed dog!

I was to get several prompts from spirit about when to trust my intuition, including the old faithful gut feeling. If my instinct was correct my solar plexus would flutter in a most comforting way; I certainly knew if my gut feeling was telling me not to do something! But the breakthrough came whilst I was driving one day.

I had been working and was between driving lessons, still searching for my intuition. I knew it was there somewhere but couldn't put my finger on it (truth is you can't put your finger on it wherein lies the problem!). I knew it was my inner voice, for want of a better description, but had not yet managed to tap into it. I decided to ask my intuition if it was there. No sooner had I finished asking the question than I heard a loud "YES" shout straight back at me from inside!

"Is that my intuition?"

"Yes"

But the response was so fast that the answer was coming at me before I'd finished asking the question.

"Is that my i...."

"Yes"

Am I hearing thi"

"No"

"Is that my"

"Yes"

The response time was so fast I was now getting answers to questions before I could speak the question. In other words I could "feel" a question but the answer was already there before I got chance to "think" about the question. It was intuitive and it was always correct!

I had another driving lesson to do so I decided to close it down.

"I'm going now, are you still there?"

"Yes"

"Go away"

"Are you still there?"

"Yes"

To say I was feeling just a little bit crazy at this point would not be far from the truth, and I did even question my sanity at the speed of thought I was having, and the speed of thought that the answers came.

So for the rest of the day I played with my new found friend and started to feel that when I was using this inner voice, I felt totally at ease and relaxed with it. And, as I started to relax more, I began to realize that I knew when things were right just because they felt right. And when they weren't right it didn't feel right! This process would continue and is still continuing today and is the basis of everything I do, including teaching people to drive.

It was now apparent that the reason for my success as a driving instructor was that, not only was I teaching people to drive, I was teaching them to work out solutions to problems intuitively and therefore a way of learning that would empower them to make the correct decisions about their lives. The only person who hadn't realized this was me!

And, as promised, now that I had found and had started to use my intuition they gave Mark his headphones back. Ann stumbled across them in a box in his bedroom that she had stored things in before she decorated. The funny thing is that the headphones were *DEFINITELY* not put there by Ann!

CHAPTER TWO
PSYCHIC DRIVING LESSONS

LEARNING TO DRIVE

So now that I had an idea about intuition, it made me realize how learning to drive is very similar to how we move along our lives. Also, the roads are the best place to learn about life because every facet of human behaviour is clearly visible every day if we care to watch it. The whole psychology of driving is just a mirror of human life and the same problems we have in driving are the same problems we face every day in various situations. I always say that a person's personality is exaggerated once they get behind the wheel. I thought I was just being an observer of human life - little did I know that I too was learning, ready for what the future had in store!

On many occasions when I have been teaching, I would ask a question such as "What are you going to do if a bus comes round that bend we are approaching?" and, sure enough on cue, a bus would suddenly appear, coming towards us, causing the pupil to panic a little (they always said they were ready but, in truth, never thought it would actually happen!).

They would ask immediately "Are you psychic?" to which I would reply "No, I've just got twenty five years' experience."

I put these occurrences down to my experience and professionalism as an instructor, as many experienced drivers would, but many of my pupils did call me "Psychic Dave!" I just smiled, totally unaware at the time that I *actually was*.

The standard perception of a driving school pupil is a seventeen year old who has been brought to you by parents to get through the driving test as quickly as possible, especially as his/her friends at school have already passed with another instructor after only a few lessons and with the minimum of fuss etc. Well, most school common rooms are full of tall stories about driving. The pupils are usually economical with the truth and like to exaggerate things like "I just nearly killed my driving instructor on the by-pass", when really they meant they had stalled at a roundabout as they were trying to get on the by-pass – embarrassing but hardly a near death experience!

This also taught me a lot about human ego, especially in a competitive environment. I had seen this throughout my life but I was now seeing it from a different viewpoint. There were schools who actually had a league table in the common room showing how many driving lessons a person had, how many attempts it took to pass and how many crashes they had, and to think, I was trying to teach these people a life saving skill and this had been brought down to the level of a game of ego - a sign of how destructive human ego can be. I would regularly meet pupils for the first time who were scared to death of learning to drive, not because of the dangers of driving, but because of the "bullying" that would start when their class mates found out they were learning. When I speak to them and tell them that my only concern is that they drive safely to protect themselves and that I really do not care about what path we take, they started to relax. As a result, they often become the good drivers in the school and will go through their early solo driving career without an incident, a different story to those who, driven by ego, had gone into their tests too early and then claimed to be good drivers. The best compliments I receive are when parents congratulate me because they feel safe whilst being driven by their children but not their children's friends.

I often hear the comment "My friend has got his test next month but I want to pass before him". I point out to them that having passed a driving test at eighteen, for example, a driving license will need to be replaced at seventy years old (barring misadventure). That is a total of fifty-two years! Now tell me seriously that an extra three or four weeks is going to make that much difference! I did have the advantage of age on my side to back that up, I can't even remember what month I passed my driving test, all I know is it was somewhere near my birthday.

So, in many peoples eyes, the seventeen year old category became lovingly known as the young and stupid category (I was young and stupid once so I should know!). There are some very responsible seventeen year olds, don't get me wrong, but maturity usually develops after the eighteenth birthday and, I am pleased to say, I have the fortune to teach all age groups.

I am aware that most of my pupils are older than seventeen, a good mix of both sexes and from lots of different backgrounds. I hear other instructors say things like "If somebody rings me with a foreign accent I tell them I'm fully booked" or "I tell them it gets harder to learn after seventeen so I tend not to take anybody older". Outrageous!

Firstly, bills have to be paid so every customer has to be seen as an income, like it or not! Secondly, I have had the pleasure of teaching some very interesting and wonderful people of whose life experiences most seventeen year olds would only have read about in a magazine. One instructor once said to me, "I notice, when I pass you on the road, that you teach all ages. If I get anybody over twenty I consider them a geriatric!".

I also seemed to attract pupils who have had some kind of difficulties in their lives. At first this seemed to be just part of the job but, as time went on, I began feeling that I wasn't here to teach driving, I was here to empower people and give them something that would kick start their lives. This is true of any person passing their driving test, but I was getting people who had severe illnesses, low self esteem, family problems, the list goes on.

Many times a driving lesson will start with me asking, "What do you know?"

"About driving?" they reply.

I say "About anything, football? Coronation Street?"

And I will be welcomed into their private lives without hesitation. It is as if the driving is the goal but to achieve that goal I have to cleanse the person of their troubles in order to focus on the job in hand. If somebody is driving badly my first job seems to be to remove the block holding them back, whether it be a relationship split, a health scare, exam worries, etc. I quite often joke that my job is sometimes that of a counselor! Many other driving instructors feel the same way but the vast majority only focus on the driving and teach in a way that suits the instructor and not the pupil. I gain many pupils from these instructors and all have the same stories.

"My instructor shouts at me when I get it wrong, he calls me stupid". I wouldn't pay for the privilege of being shouted at, if I do ever raise my voice to anybody it is to get a point across and only when necessary.

"My instructor made me drive through town on my second lesson and I didn't like it so I thought I must be rubbish and I gave up. That was seven years ago". Of course they didn't like it! Talk about throwing somebody in at the deep end! Some people love to be chucked in but here we are in a killing machine in a town full of people with a driver who is scared and doesn't know what they are doing because things are happening so fast around them, WOAH STOP!

Obviously the pupil thinks they should be better and other people never complain about this so they think that they must be rubbish and their confidence is crushed when actually, they should never have been put in that situation by the thoughtless instructor. Confidence comes from doing things right then builds up hand in hand with the skills. This poor pupil has wasted seven years when they could have been driving.

"My instructor kept stopping for a cigarette break during the lesson. He offered me a cigarette but I don't smoke". Yes this actually happens! If the pupil has asked to stop for a cigarette or a break then that is different, it is their money. There is a standard of professionalism that is needed if you are going to teach somebody a difficult and dangerous skill. The amount of times I see instructors at the test centre looking unkempt and scruffy. Then they wonder why their pupils treat them like second-rate mates, letting them down with lessons and payments.

If you want to be a professional, look like a professional! I wear a shirt and trousers during office hours then tee shirt and jeans outside these times. I don't go with the whole suit thing - I did that in the motor trade - but it is amazing how much respect I get from pupils, examiners and other instructors just because I look right.

Always remember that the pupil is paying, but what for?

The obvious answer is to learn to drive, but I have had pupils who believe that I should pick them up and immediately let them drive without stopping for a full hour then get out and go home. In other words they've paid for an hour so they will drive for *exactly one hour*! If this happens then how will they know what is expected of them? What chance have I got to explain any new skills or to correct what is going wrong?

The art of stopping, standing back and contemplating is a valuable one. Now am I talking driving instruction or spiritual instruction here? The answer is both. You can see how the two are linked and, without realizing it, I was already teaching the art of contemplation!

Of course people pay for driving lessons but actually what they are getting is more. It is a friendly face, it is a chat, it is a chance to run things by somebody else, a chance to learn about life!

On more than one occasion I have helped young people write their CV. I have taught them interview techniques including how to dress and how to impress. In my past career I have interviewed many members of staff and I know what works.

I have helped people to come to terms with illness, including depression and anxiety. Low self-esteem is sometimes just a fear of learning something new because the feeling is that everybody else on the road knows what they are doing. I do assure them that this is sadly not the case, but if we recognize the things that could go wrong then we can avoid the bad things. Low self-esteem can also be a condition of the mind and it is amazing how these people ever get the courage to pick up a phone and call me in the first place. Yet, having made the call they only want somebody who can hold their hand and guide them through the steps we need to take in order to achieve a certain goal. Am I talking driving or spirituality? Again it's both.

There are, of course, the people for whom a driving lesson is not about driving at all. It is a chance to escape normal daytime routine and have an hour a week where there is a chance to talk, laugh, swear, and have fun! We spend quite a few hours with our pupils and, in some ways, it is always a sad day when they pass their driving test! We might bump into each other again in the future (not literally, hopefully) but apart from that it marks the end of a path.

Quite often a pupil will say to me "I don't know what I'm going to do without my hour with you when I pass" and they will genuinely mean it. Of course, some of them don't want to pass for this reason and if I feel they are dragging their feet I will say "Come on, I need to get rid of you – in the nicest possible way, of course!"

People often come into our lives for just a short time and leave their mark by teaching us something. Although I like to think that I am that person to them, I always do know that they are that person to me. I thank them all for the things they have taught me, some of which will help me to explain my path.

THE DREADED "PART 3"

If anybody knows the path to becoming a driving instructor in the UK they will know the cloud that is the dreaded "Part 3"!

"Part 1" is a one hundred question theory test covering all aspects a learner driver needs to know. It also includes legal issues, different ways of training and lots of facts and figures. A high pass mark is required and I passed this at the first attempt.

"Part 2" is next and is a test of your driving ability. I did this in Sale, Manchester, and again passed at the first attempt.

"Part 3" is the final and most difficult hurdle. This is a test of instructional ability and is judged on several criteria including control of lesson, the subject being taught, the ability to identify faults, analyze them and correct them. It takes the form of two driving lessons with an examiner in role-play, each one lasting half an hour. For the first lesson they assume the role of a learner who is near the beginning of their lessons and not very experienced. They explain the pupil they are role-playing then give you the subject they would like you to teach. For the second hour they assume a different pupil who is well on their way along the road to test standard.

Fitting all the information into a half hour driving lesson is difficult enough but the examiner makes it more difficult by throwing you problems to deal with whilst they are driving. Hence the dreaded "Part 3" earns its title and is where most people fail to qualify. Once "Part 2" is passed you have two years in which to pass "Part 3", but only three attempts. If you fail all three or your time expires then you have to wait two years before beginning the whole process again.

Having just walked out of the Motor Trade and having done some training for this job I decided that I should try and qualify as soon as possible, so I booked an appointment at Sale. Having been a trainer in my last jobs I thought I would be well prepared.

A lady examiner accompanied me to my car and explained what she had done and what she wanted me to teach her. I explained the subject and asked her to drive on when she was ready. I wasn't prepared for what happened next, as I thought an experienced examiner would show some common sense, but she pulled away and started accelerating towards a crossroads where we had to give way! I immediately used my dual controls to stop her from going across the junction until we had looked properly and then continued the lesson, followed by the next lesson.

At the end we had a chat and she told me I had failed only because I had used the dual controls at the beginning. If it wasn't for that, I would have passed. Welcome to "Part 3", the trainee driving instructors graveyard!

I went back to the franchise I was working for and they gave me some extra training in Lincoln, where my instructor was based. He was a retired Supervising Driving Examiner and a really friendly and helpful man. Despite this he knew Part "3" inside out and every trick in the book. He would try everything to throw me off guard, making sure I was on the ball and didn't miss a thing.

So I went for my second attempt, at Lincoln this time. The examiner came out and introduced him self and described who he was role playing and what he wanted me to teach.

As he went to move away he didn't check his blind spots, so I stopped him and asked him to make sure he checked them.

"What for?" he shouted.

Here we go, an examiner trick, so I explained that there could be somebody standing near the car and it would be better just to check etc.

"There's nobody there"

"Have you checked?"

"No"

"Then how do you know"

This was all very silly now and was out of order. He had made the error deliberately, I had spotted it and made him aware so he needed to correct it and move on. But he didn't, he kept arguing!

The whole hour was conducted in the same manner; he was so rude and difficult. My confidence sank and I knew I had become a victim of the dreaded "Part 3". After the test he explained that I should have just ignored him and let him continue without checking his blind spots.

WHAT? I can hear the groan from every driving instructor reading this!

I reported back to my franchise company who couldn't believe it and added that they had concerns about this examiner from another candidate so they advised me to report him to the Driving Standards Agency.

I did this and received the standard reply about the conduct of the test and that the examiner claimed I was in the wrong. Funny how they are always sent back for re-training though!

I now had a problem. I only had one attempt left but I had quit my job and if I didn't pass this time then I was effectively unemployed. I was teaching on a trainee license but that was dependent on me passing "Part 3". The other issue I had was that I just didn't know what was needed to pass and when I asked other driving instructors, neither did they!

I bit the bullet and booked my third and final attempt, again at Lincoln. It was January and had been snowing on and off. As I drove over the Pennines there was plenty of snow about and I wondered what it would be like at the test center. I stopped and rang them to ask.

"Oh yes the test is still on at the moment". Great, my final attempt and to make it more difficult it was snowing. All I would need now is to get the same examiner! I sat in the Test Centre waiting room and the door opened for the examiners to enter.

It was him! I might as well give up now! A feeling of impending doom seemed to be in the air but something stronger took over. I suddenly had the thought that I was going to do this test exactly how I believed it should be done, stuff the training, stuff the fear of failure, stuff what the examiner thought, this was going to be the DAVID SMITH School of Motoring way!

We walked to the car and he told me he was called Fred and explained the lesson he wanted me to teach him. As he proceeded to drive away, he hadn't checked his blind spots.

Here we go again! Do I let it go as he suggested last time or do I pull him up on it as my instinct and training told me to?

"Stop"

"Why"

"You haven't checked your blind spots"

"Why do I need to do that?"

"There may be somebody standing there that you can't see"

"There isn't"

"It will take two seconds to check so just do it"

Reluctantly he looked and we continued.

This time I had a good feeling about the way things were going. I was doing it my way and I just didn't care!

We were stopped at a set of red traffic lights and he let out a huge sigh.

"What's wrong Fred"

"Driving is tiring isn't it?"

"It is. Are you enjoying it, though?"

"Oh I'm loving it"

The lights changed and we moved on. We returned to the test centre and he went away to deliberate. I sat in the waiting room, nervously contemplating my fate until he called me in.

In his office he told me I had passed and that they had been two excellent driving lessons. The grades he gave me were really high and I couldn't believe it was the same examiner. He told me I had a really nice way of teaching which made me angry that he had been so awkward on the last attempt, otherwise he may have seen that then.

I left him and phoned Ann to tell her.

"I did it!" I wasn't so much elated as exhausted and, for days after, Ann and I would say to each other "I/ You did it!"

And the thing that got me through in the end was following my intuition all the time.

My intuition was to help me on my check test too. Again I decided to ignore the many training aids available and just do what I thought was necessary.

A driving instructor is check tested every so often to make sure they are still at the required standard to teach. A Supervising Examiner sits in the back of the car while you give a one hour driving lesson. The criteria is the same as on a Part Three test but the situation is more true to life as you have a real pupil to work with and it is one chosen by the instructor.

I had chosen to do pedestrian crossings with a pupil who could benefit from this. We exchanged all the pleasantries and the pupil drove through the town, on a route I had planned, while I explained what we were looking for and how to approach.

We pulled up at the side of the road and I said to him "Now you know what we're looking for I'm going to shut up and let you get on with it. I'll give you directions but you're in charge now"

He looked surprised but he drove well and we discussed where he could have improved before driving back to the test centre. The examiner discussed it with me and gave me high grades saying I was just one mark off the top grade, Doh! Then she said, "You have an amazing way of transferring information, it's so natural!"

So, by following what I felt, I was able to get high grades without a lot of effort, yet if I followed the training and advice available I suffered badly! As if to confirm this, the Check Test is now marked on the ability of the Instructor to teach in a customer centred way instead of the old traditional way of following strict disciplines. I rest the case for following your intuition because, at the end of the day, your intuition is never wrong!

GUARDIAN ANGEL

We all have a Guardian Angel, don't we? The idea that we are born with a life plan and a path to tread is a fairly common idea with Spiritualists, but when we come to earth we are all given free will to do what the hell we want anyway! So what is the job of a Guardian Angel?

My understanding of the job of a Guardian Angel is to make sure we keep to the path we are supposed to be on. But if we are to use our free will then that gives us scope to travel off it from time to time, otherwise how we will we learn as we go through our lives? I suppose the Guardian Angel is there to make sure that, having learnt about things we shouldn't be involved with, they can bring us back to where we should be so that we can get on with what we should be learning about.

This includes near death experiences, those times when the crash is so severe that nobody can survive yet people just walk away from it. You can imagine the Guardian Angel looking on and saying "It's not your time yet, mate" before grabbing that person and removing them from the impact before returning them safely after the crash!

I have had two such instances. I know it is widely thought that I risk life and limb every day whilst teaching, but the fact is that most of my teaching is done in a controlled way and the pupil is taught risk assessment and how to reduce the risk (or at least that is what should be taught). I did see a Driving Instructor at the test centre once with a tee shirt that said in bold letters, "**YOU DON'T FRIGHTEN ME, I'M A DRIVING INSTRUCTOR**"!

I was taking a lady who had already passed her driving test for a refresher lesson, as she had crashed her car a week after passing. It was only a small crash but it had knocked her confidence and she hadn't driven afterwards but now needed to for her job. It is common for people to lose confidence quickly and refresher lessons are a good way of boosting it back up, especially as all the skills are already there.

We had done about four lessons and she was now feeling good again. This was the last of her agreed lessons and we stopped at a set of red traffic lights and waited.

I will explain the scenario. We were going ahead at the lights and nobody was behind us. Opposite was a car waiting to turn, crossing our path. The crossroad was blind so we could not see the lights or the traffic to the left or right. On the pavement were two young girls about sixteen years old. The lights changed to red/amber then green, but as they did, the two girls started to cross the road. Quite often when young people do this in modern Britain there is a touch of arrogance and a defiant look from the people crossing but this was different. These girls were just wandering across the road in a non-aggressive way when one of them turned and looked me in the eye. She looked as if she didn't know why she was crossing the road and, as our eyes met, there was a look of oneness, as if time had just stood still.

Normally in this situation the driver opposite would have used the time to turn across us and get out of the way but she stayed where she was. Reality soon struck when a car appeared from the left and sped straight across the lights while their lights were on red! There was no slowing down or sign of caution from the driver, the car looked like it was doing thirty miles per hour and the driver must have assumed his light was green! If we had been able to go we would have had a very serious collision on my side and the consequences could have been fatal.

The girls crossed and we continued. The woman I was teaching looked surprised and said "I think somebody was looking after us then" to which I thought, "If only you knew!" I could imagine the opposite driver saying to her husband later "You'll never guess what happened today?"

When I was at home that night I had the chance to contact my Guardian Angel who confirmed she had used the girls to stop us going. But I couldn't understand why the other driver didn't take advantage and go. I was immediately shown a picture of the situation with a huge angel hovering above the traffic lights, one hand on our bonnet and one hand on the bonnet of the car opposite. A car sped though the lights then the angel released the bonnets and all went ahead as normal.

I will never forget the look in the eyes of that girl. She will never realize what had happened, it's as if she had been asleep for that short time, but it was a look I would see many times after that event when spirit makes contact between two people. After all, the eyes are the windows of the soul.

Another time I was driving with a young man who had problems with low self esteem. He is a nice guy but falls apart if something goes wrong and then we need to spend the next few minutes trying to restore his confidence. We were driving along and he was doing really well. I was very relaxed with his driving. I suddenly heard a buzzing in my ear as if somebody was trying to get my attention. I tuned in and it was my Guardian Angel telling me to be careful. Strange, I thought, nothing seemed likely to go wrong, in fact his driving couldn't be better.

We approached a staggered crossroads and had to stop at the Give Way line. To get across we had to turn into the new road, which was wide enough to wait in, before turning across the oncoming traffic into the road opposite. The first road was wide enough to turn into and wait to complete the move by crossing the traffic but a blind bend made it impossible to see what was coming, so it was a dangerous cross.

He set off and, without warning and completely surprising himself, accelerated into the middle, losing control and ending up on the wrong side of the road facing a blind bend and stopped. If anything came quickly towards us it would have hit us head on. I immediately adopted emergency driving instructor mode and calmly told him what to do to get the car into the side road and out of danger.

We pulled up at the side of the road and switched the engine off. He apologized and couldn't believe what he had just done, it was so out of character with the drive he had just had. He then started to tell me how his sleep patterns have been badly affected by working nights, and the fact that he has had glandular fever and has never fully recovered. He is not the first pupil to suddenly come out with a random issue that I have had to discuss (all part of being a light worker I suppose!).

I have had glandular fever and I know it can take months, sometimes years to regain full strength, so I was able to help him to understand that it was not his fault if his sleep was disrupted and that there may be things he can do to help, such as speak to his friend who he told me practices yoga. I cannot really explain to my pupils that I am a light worker and count spiritual healing and medium ship amongst the things I have done! But what I can do is push them in a direction where they can find the answers for themselves and feel empowered that they have conquered their problem. I do also ask for healing from the angels so they can be guided correctly.

So do I believe in angels? *YES*. But I am lucky for I have seen them in action and they are extremely impressive when they get going! Do not rely on them to cure stupidity, though. If you deliberately drive your car into a tree to test this theory they will probably save your life but leave you to live it with your broken body, for we are here to learn after all!

A GREATER INTELLIGENCE

I quite often get calls from parents who are eager for their unruly and ungrateful offspring to be taught the proper way to drive hoping it knocks some sense into them! There was one parent, though, who seemed to know what she wanted from the start, and time would prove her to be right. She contacted me for her son and we agreed the time and place – her house on the council estate where she lived.

I arrived on time, as usual, to be welcomed by her but with the news that her son wasn't there and she was trying to get hold of him. He had gone to another town with his mates but had been held up on his way back, making him late for his first lesson. This was a two hour beginner lesson and was planned that way so it can be a chilled and relaxed way of introducing a person to driving. That was the plan but time was ticking away and I was aware that this could turn into a rushed and stressful lesson and defeat the object of the two hours.

His Mum and I talked about this and that and had a nice chat. I was keeping an eye on the clock to make sure the lesson wasn't going to end up rushed and pointless, but I got the feeling she was trying to hang on to me and stop me going.

As usual, in a situation like this, I left to get on with my day, asking her to contact me again if she wanted to re-book. The customer then decides either to call me back full of apologies and we begin again, or they decide it was not for them or feel too embarrassed and I don't get the call. As I drove away from the house my phone rang but I couldn't answer it as I was driving, so I pulled to a safe place and checked who it was. It was her phone number so I called her back and, sure enough, her son had just returned home and she was pleading with me to come back. The lesson time was now reduced to just under one and a half hours, which she accepted, so I went back.

There he was, really apologetic, and straight out of one car into mine. I drove him away and started asking about himself so I could gauge a picture of what kind of person I was dealing with. As he spoke, he came across as a nice and responsible young man who was thinking of going to college to train in Public Service. We completed the shorter lesson and arranged some more but this time from his new home off the council estate which he was relieved about. Like I said, he was a responsible man and all too aware of some of the pitfalls of where he had moved from. As I was brought up on a council estate myself, I knew exactly what pros and cons there were.

He developed well and we got to know each other through the training. His Mum was a single mother and had other children, all younger than my pupil. I knew she had been in hospital but I never asked why and was never told. Not everybody told me their life story and that was their choice; it wasn't for me to find out unless they offered it.

I occasionally turn up for a pupil's driving lesson only to find the house empty, so I try all their phone numbers, wait for fifteen minutes then leave a card through the door with their next appointment on it. I also write a little note on the card telling them to get in touch with me if there is a problem and that this lesson would be chargeable because of short notice. I do have a heart so can always waive the fee if it turns out to be an emergency. I usually find out they have forgotten or have been called in to work or college, just as he had done a couple of times.

One such time this happened and it looked as if he had just been called into college again, so I wrote the note telling him it was chargeable and drove home for an unexpected cup of tea. While I was at home the phone rang and it was his Grandma.

She said "I just want to tell you why he wasn't there for his driving lesson today. His Mum died last night". I felt awful. At his time of need I had posted a demand for money through his door. I expressed my sadness and obviously told her there was no charge for the lesson.

Usually when people have a break in their driving lessons it is very hard for them to get started again and time drifts and things get forgotten, so I never see them again in a driving capacity. Knowing this I took him out of my diary and used his slot to teach other people.

I was surprised when I got a call from him only two weeks later. He asked if his normal slot was available for the next day. He sounded determined and was disappointed when I told him it had been filled. I did promise to keep it free from the week after, though, and we agreed to start again.

I remember thinking that this was somebody special. He was the eldest child and needed to drive so that he could become the figurehead and be able to take his new young family to wherever they needed to be.

I went to his house and could tell he was apprehensive and there was a misty look in his eye. We got in the car and I said to him "There is nothing I can say that can change anything but what I can do is help you with your driving. I understand your situation and if you need anything then just say so"

He appreciated this and then said, "Thanks. I know my Mum is with me and this is what she wanted me to do so I know she will help me with it". I thought "This guy is so spiritually mature for his age" and so we recommenced his driving lessons but with a new determination.

We were doing a driving lesson and approached a roundabout where a funeral procession was coming from the right. We should give way to the right in the UK but in truth the procession was going slowly and had it been any other vehicle there would have been time to make progress without upsetting it. We both agreed it would be better to wait so he came to a stop. As the hearse approached he immediately took off his beanie hat and placed it on his lap. When the hearse passed he put his hat back on and we continued driving. As we were driving away from the roundabout he said, "Would you believe at my Mum's funeral somebody overtook and ended up having to move back in between the funeral cars!" As I have said, this was a responsible young man who was ahead of his years in attitude.

It was during a meditation that his Mum appeared, smiling. I said to her "There was a reason you wouldn't let me go, wasn't there?" She said, "Yes, you are the one." I had received this message from several spirits over the months as if they were trying to build up my confidence – I needed it! But this seemed more personal. It was as if this was planned all along, even before the driving lessons were booked.

His first driving test came along and I went to collect him an hour before, as is usual for a driving test. He appeared and was probably one of the most nervous pupils I have ever seen before a driving test. I couldn't help feeling that he needed his Mum to give him a big hug and tell him he would be alright, just like other Mums when I'd collected their children for a test. But there was nobody there for him, only me. We did the drive around and got him to the test centre almost in silence. I stayed professional but all the time kept an eye on him looking for signs that he might need more support than the usual test candidate. I suppose I was the nearest thing to his Mum for that day.

He left for the test and I waited for him to return, which he did, looking drained. He had passed with flying colours. This wasn't an arms in the air celebration, this was the realization of an amazing achievement, barely weeks after his Mum had died.

I drove him back home and when we pulled up outside his house I asked him "When you said you knew your Mum was with you, you knew she was there didn't you?" and he replied with the most amazing story.

He said, "Yesterday I went to my Mum's grave to spend some time there. I picked up one of the stones from it and took it home. Last night I took the stone from my pocket and held it in my hand, looking at it. As I did all the lights flickered in the house and everybody in the house ran around wondering what was happening. Then everything went back to normal again." There he was with the stone in his hand, twiddling it between his fingers as he told me the story, with a heavy satisfied smile.

He went away to start his new life of being the family taxi, still troubled by his experience but also strengthened by it.

He is a remarkable young man.

FIRST IMPRESSIONS?

Many people send their children to me and claim their offspring will only let certain people into their trust. One such pupil was thirty six and had been suffering from schizophrenic illness for many years. His Mum was a friend of the family although I had never met him before. He had been given the go-ahead to learn to drive by his doctor and this was a big thing for him.

I turned up at their house and met him for the first time. Here was a totally charming and well-mannered man. Nothing would give you the idea he had all those problems in his life, except for his size. Because of his medications over the years he was now twenty-seven stone and not as mobile as the average thirty six year old. Despite this he was still able to walk around town quite happily and to the various clubs and groups he was involved in.

So we started his driving lessons and he progressed reasonably well. I was always aware of his past and always conscious of pushing him but not so far that he would feel under too much pressure - after all I didn't know how he would react.

We would always start the driving lesson the same way – with a discussion of what we had been doing during the last week. He liked rock music (like me), going to the theatre and the cinema and eating out at restaurants. I always seemed to have things on the go that interested him, so the first ten or fifteen minutes would be spent catching up on things!

At the beginning of one lesson we discussed the full moon. I had said that I knew it was a full moon because everybody seems to act a little stranger than normal on the roads. He replied "the moon does have an effect on people and in Victorian times people like me would have been put in an asylum because, of course, lunatic comes form the word lunar, meaning moon!" This was a man who was intelligent and a real gentle giant.

The lessons went on and he improved. Still I would watch for signs of stress in case he was being put under any undue pressure but he seemed to handle things well. I started to talk to him about a driving test and suggested he went to do his theory test, which was necessary before taking a practical test. He agreed and said he would start learning for it. Each week I would push him about his theory and he would say he was going to get it done, but I got the feeling he was stalling, there was a nervousness and unease about it. I have taught people with dyslexia before who have been really scared of the theory test. They have always passed but it really has stressed them out. I felt that he wasn't confident about it but, despite my offers of help, he kept assuring me he was on the case.

It was the early Bank Holiday Monday in May and, as it was a nice day, we had gone to a Craft Fair for some of the day. We got home and I had to go out for a while, I'm not sure where but I was on my own. I arrived home and when I walked in the door I saw Ann leaning with her back against the sink looking at me with a tear in her eye. I asked her what was wrong.

She told me he had died.

"No, he has a driving lesson tomorrow"

"His Dad has just rang up and said he had a seizure this afternoon and died"

He had had a seizure at home and was taken into hospital where he seemed to briefly recover but then passed away. His Mum was distraught. Her whole reason to live had just disappeared and she still struggles to come to terms with this.

Ann and I attended the funeral. The Vicar talked about his life and then mentioned, "He had begun driving lessons and enjoyed them very much. He loved his chats with his Driving Instructor and it gave him a whole new lease of life"

Sometimes somebody comes into your life to make a difference. I obviously made a difference to his life for a short time. He made a difference to mine forever.

I did speak to him from the spirit world during a meditation. He appeared in a sweet shop buying sweets and was very happy. He said "It's great up here I can do all the things I couldn't down there and I'm learning to drive again. Tell my Mother there's only one of me now!" I told his Mother but all she wanted was for him to contact her and let her know he was alright. The truth is that he is with her all the time and he is alright. His Mum is the one who is suffering but that is the hard part of passing, it is the ones who are left behind who do the suffering. The deceased are now free to pursue their spiritual path without the constraints of a physical world to hold them back or give them pain.

DENIAL

One of my pupils was a seventeen year old boy living with his Dad and his Dad's partner. His Dad was well mannered and lovely to talk to but Gordon was different. To say he was out of touch with reality would be unfair, but there was something very strange from the outset. He was difficult to converse with because he would only speak in sentences of two or three quickly spoken words. When I called at his house he would open the door and grunt, like a lot of teenagers do, but his manner was completely different. Quite often he would have bits of food stuck in his teeth and in his brace. He was like a spinning top, never still, and when I gave him the car keys he would grab them and run across his front lawn to the car like a six year old. I did tell him on one occasion to say "thank you". He would get in the car and immediately want to drive without doing any cockpit checks. When I mentioned it, he would look at me and give one of those "I am so forgetful" looks that an older person would give, but he would slap his hand onto his forehead in his usual excited way! When he tried to pull away he invariably left the handbrake on or forgot to put it into gear and again would show his feeling of foolishness in his own inimitable way.

We had quite a few driving lessons and I was really struggling. I would try and get him to look for hazards and teach him how to deal with them but there seemed to be no common sense in what he was doing. His Dad would tell me how he was taking his son out and letting him drive very challenging routes with some very challenging junctions yet I could never get him off his estate without him putting us in danger by sudden braking, or being on the wrong side of the road, or trying to accelerate out of a junction into other traffic! When I asked him about driving with his Dad he confirmed that lots of people had been sounding their horns at him and he'd kept stalling but his Dad would always talk as if nothing was wrong.

The driving just wasn't improving and every week I would start the lesson with the intention of pushing him further but was always held back by his apparent lack of awareness. I tried to get an opportunity to talk with his Dad alone but it was difficult to separate them. When I did manage to get him alone I would ask if there was anything I should know about his son, anything that would help me to understand him better. It was now obvious to me he had some kind of autism but his Dad just kept treating him like any other child. I fully understand his point, as society has built up a picture of what is normal and what is not, but if we all examine ourselves we will find that we all have parts of us that would be considered not normal. But if I knew what his issues were I would be able to adjust the teaching, as I had done for others before. I was being met with a wall of denial.

I really felt for my pupil. He was being led along, totally oblivious to life around him, yet he had so much enthusiasm and energy to give. If only the people around him could accept him for what he was and adjust life slightly to accommodate him then everybody would benefit and be happier with it.

I asked my pendulum several questions the night before his next lesson.

Are there learning difficulties – Yes
Is he autistic – Yes
Does his father know – Yes

I was surprised by this and felt angry at first that his Dad was letting him down.

Does his Mother know – Yes

Is his father trying to ignore it – Yes

Is he happy about it – No

Does he need help - Yes

Am I teaching him correctly – No

I was surprised by this answer but was keen to know how I could change it for him. Then a thought came into my mind

Do I have to keep things very simple – Yes

So I started thinking about how simple to keep it.

Would the angels help me to teach him – Yes

The next day I picked him up as usual and he seemed quieter, a bit subdued and he walked to the car, he didn't run. He sat in the car and did his cockpit drill, then we drove away under complete control but I could sense this was a different person than the one I knew. I kept my commands simple. Instead of "I would like you to take the next road on the left" I would say slowly "turn left". It seemed a bit short and rude but he responded well. I would add, "make sure you give yourself enough time" and he would slow down and do it perfectly.

He drove so well I decided to extend the route off his estate. In fact he drove so well that he drove all through the town centre, round lots of roundabouts and dealt with many difficult traffic situations, some of which I had not taught him. But here was a different person, able to keep calm, think and work out difficult problems for himself. He barely made a sound, so different from the normal series of grunts and exclamations he would normally make. This child was suddenly a young adult.

I finished the lesson and was stunned. I drove round the corner on the way to my next call and stopped to get out my pendulum.

Did that really happen – Yes
Was somebody helping – Yes
Were they helping me – No
Were they helping my pupil – Yes
Was it any of his family members – No
Was it the Angels – Yes

If I wasn't on the path I was on I wouldn't have believed it and would have hailed it as a miracle but I was just left with a feeling of awe and wonderment at how the angels had come in to help him.

I received a phone call a week later from his Dad saying that he felt his son was not progressing enough and that it might be time to change instructor. We discussed it in a civilized way, as I always do, but I could not handle my frustration that this young man was now starting to shine with the help of the angels and I was going to lose him. My frustration also went so far as to ask his Dad for some honesty. Still he denied there was a problem with his son and believed that if he banged his head against enough walls then he would get the result he was after. Maybe he will, I thought, but not before he has fractured his skull. I convinced him to keep his last appointment with me and even offered him the chance to sit in the back which, unsurprisingly, he declined.

We had that last driving lesson and I started it by saying, "This is our last driving lesson so I just want you to drive like you did last week".

To my surprise he said, "My Dad's decided it is my last one" but there was a genuine look of sadness in his eyes and I could feel his soul touching mine. I told him that he knew where I was if he needed me.

Again the drive was of a maturity well ahead of his behaviour and I enjoyed every minute of it. At the end I wished him every success and drove off feeling that my heart had been touched by this awkward boy's inner self. I prayed for healing for both he and his Dad, and felt at peace with situation. We had all learnt a lot.

I still see him, occasionally, as he walks to college and around town. When I see him we make eye contact and smile. It is a smile between souls but to the outside world it is just a strange boy smiling at a strange driving instructor!

EGO

As a driving instructor I have two heads - not literally, obviously! I have my teaching head that is tuned into the person I am teaching. I also have my business head, which is when I look at the money, how full is my diary, the running costs, of which there are many, and whether the family can eat at Christmas!

It is the business side that brings out the worst in peoples ego and mine used to be the same. If anybody criticized my style of teaching I was offended. If anybody said I was too pricey I was offended. If anybody left me I was offended. Spirit taught me a valuable lesson about ego in the most spectacular way.

I had been teaching a girl who worked in a corporate office during the day so she would have evening lessons. I would pick her up from where she lived and every week was the same.

The problem sometimes with corporate offices is that ego determines what the result of an exercise is before deciding how to do it. How many times have people promised you something only to find out that what they have promised you is not possible? Also, there is a misconception that if you throw money at something it will work better. To give you an example, if you pay an athlete $100 to run one hundred metres then he will do it in a certain time. If you pay him $1000 he should run it ten times faster! More money does not always equate to better performance, a lesson society has to learn as we always blame the failure of services and football teams on lack of money!

So here she was, singing from the corporate hymn sheet. She knew the standard she wanted to get to but had no idea how to achieve it.

Enter me! I would help her to understand what she needed to do in step-by-step chunks just like the training books suggest, but would she listen? As I explained things she would give me the corporate nod and continually talk over the training in the way I have seen in my previous jobs. The result being that when she started to drive she would be all over the place from the start! When I tried to correct her she would agree and talk over the instruction I was giving her with "I know" so she completely missed the point of what I was saying.

In truth, she was having problems driving in a straight line and not slowing down approaching hazards, sometimes not even realizing there was a hazard there, blinded by her own inflated view of the standard she was at. She lived in the middle of town and there was no way I would have let her drive from home because of her lack of ability, but as the lessons were at night the roads were quiet so the danger was somewhat reduced.

I trusted her, but still with trepidation, allowing her to drive from her house on a route I had chosen to minimize any heavy traffic. She would then drive back and finish the lesson totally oblivious to the poor driving she had done.

At the end of one lesson she complained that I wasn't giving her enough driving time and that it was interrupted by me stopping her to train her. So how am I going to train somebody if I just allow them to drive badly and not correct them? Also, the stopping time was a chance to get our breath back. If she thought a new subject would just magically be taught without having to think about it then I'm sorry, I might be psychic but telepathic I am still working on!

I told her that she is actually getting more driving than she probably should because I have worked a route for her to drive from home. Normally for people like her I would drive them to a local training area and let them drive back. It saves time if I drive and also avoids the problems like we were having. However, she would have none of that – "corporate ego"

So here we had a pupil who would not listen to instruction or training, could not really handle the driving we were doing but wanted me to let her do more driving.

I was cleaning my car at the weekend and I received a phone call. It was her and she was telling me she did not want any more driving lessons with me because she felt I should be giving her more driving to do and not to keep stopping to train her!

I WAS ANGRY!

I was polite to her but when I put the phone down I spent a good hour cursing her and going over and over in my mind how stupid she was and ignorant of how bad she really was.

I know what you're thinking – forgive and forget! – Not a chance.

While I was in this state my family informed me there was no hot water. As if I wasn't angry enough! I checked the boiler and everything was ok, but no hot water. Typical! I couldn't find anything wrong so left it thinking it would be a callout for the plumber.

That night I went to play football (Sunday night treat) and came home for a shower. Still no hot water and there I was all sweaty from playing football. I bit the bullet and showered with cold water and, yes, it was uncomfortable! I went downstairs and was still seething at this woman.

I got a feeling that a meditation was in order so I lit a candle and started to relax. The flame flickered merrily along guided by spirit and I went into my inner space. This was the most relaxed I had felt all day. I pondered. I was at the stage in my development where I was being told to use my intuition so I tried to find it.

When I finished I stood up and thought about the boiler. I went over to the fuse box and, sure enough, the thirty amp fuse had tripped. I switched it back on and we had hot water! ***Doh!***

It was at the time when spirit were moving and controlling things around our house to make us aware and to set tasks - but tripping the switch? Thanks!

The next night I demanded answers from spirit. Sure enough this was a lesson they were teaching me. Of course the pupil didn't listen and was unreasonable, I wasn't the one who was in the wrong but I should just let it go. If you hang on to negativity it will only bring you down, as it did.

And what about the hot water? How else could they get my attention in the state I was in?

It was all to teach me a lesson that, at the end of the day, although I complained about her ego then mine was just as big if not bigger.

Just let it go and move on!

DIAMOND

Admit it, the usual perception of an angel is a robe wearing, harp playing pacifist whose only pleasure in life is preening their wings on a cloud! If I have learned anything over the years then I have learned never to judge things on the first impression because it will only lead to disappointment.

I first came into contact with one pupil when she and her friend would come to driving lessons together and I would do their lesson one at a time while the other sat in the back. As time went on her friend moved away so she was left on her own.

I don't want to give too much away but she was the kind of person I had seen a lot of on the council estate, the type of person your Mother would try and keep you away from. She had a hard upbringing, always missing school, went through difficult periods and was a single mother to several children. Many women would have crumbled but not her.

She stopped having her driving lessons because, as she put it, "I got drunk and fell asleep on the bus and when I woke up somebody had stolen my purse with my driving license in it and I thought stuff it!" or words to that effect!

After that, I used to see her walking round while I was teaching and every time I saw her she seemed to have added another child. We used to joke through the open car window when it was sunny,

"How many have you got now?"

"Five"

"You just don't know when to stop do you?"

After a few years I got a call from her to start driving lessons again and was surprised when she said "I didn't know whether to ring because I didn't know whether you would want to teach me again". I never turn anybody away but she is one of those pupils who would guarantee to raise a smile during every lesson.

She was driving down a national speed limit country road during one lesson and an articulated lorry started to pull out of a side road while we were doing forty to fifty miles per hour. Instead of the usual panic and "What do I do?" question, she calmly checked behind and started braking early giving the lorry plenty of time to pull out and get away. At the end of the lesson I asked her, "What are you particularly pleased about today?".

Her reply, "I'm dead pleased because this week I got you out of the s*** instead of putting you in it like I normally do!"

She now had five children and was as a single mother She was on benefits because she couldn't work, such was the range of the ages of the children. Yet as the lessons began again she revealed a side that I hadn't seen before.

At the beginning of each lesson she would tell me what had gone wrong that week and how the children were winding her up and she was having trouble with the neighbours, some of whom were not particularly nice.

It was easy to judge her by the way she looked and behaved but not many people got the insight into her mind that I did. Inside she had a heart of gold and would always want to do the right thing by people. Although she would moan about her children she would tell me how she always made sure they had enough food in the house even if it meant not eating herself. She would budget for Christmas months in advance so they would not go without presents. Yet if any of her children stepped out of line she was the first to administer strict discipline and make it known that this bevaviour was not acceptable. While other kids in the area were running riot and always up to no good she would rather keep her children at home where she knew where they were and couldn't get into trouble.

All of this was because she knew what life was like at the bottom, having lived that way for years and did not want her children to struggle as she had done.

She cared about her extended family, even though she admitted that they had come to grief because of their own fault. She was always the first to respond when anybody needed a safe haven to recover or escape to in times of trouble. She would go to extraordinary lengths to make things happen because she always saw the good in people and wanted to lead them into a better way of living, whether that meant looking after them or giving them a kick up the back side when necessary!

So there was this single mother looking after several children in sheltered housing but sacrificing everything for them, even though to the outside world she was a battle hardened woman who could argue and hold her own. But she also had a vulnerable side.

She would often say "I'll be dangerous when I pass my test and I don't think I'll ever be ready". For all her bravado there was a fear of the unknown.

Her first test came and she didn't pass, only through loss of concentration, so we planned another.

This time it was snowing when we turned up at the test centre so it was cancelled. It wasn't a complete surprise and she looked at me and said "Come on, I'll buy you a coffee". We went to a café round the corner and she paid, despite having already paid me for the lesson and me trying to tell her I would pay. We talked about family life and there was a calm as we talked. I realized this was a special woman, not in the conventional way, but take her away from the troubles at home, and she had an inner light that seemed to glow.

She booked another test and it was cancelled again due to the snow. Again she bought me coffee and we talked. Again there was the same feeling.

She booked her fourth test and this time it went ahead. She was under strict instructions to "shut up and concentrate" as the connection between talking and losing concentration had been found to be the problem! She did and she passed.

It was clear she did not want these lessons to finish as it was her way of leaving the life she had for an hour and talking to a listening ear, perhaps the ear that she had never been able to find in a partner.

She surprised me by asking me to find her on Facebook. I only used Facebook for family and friends at that time. Several of my pupils have asked me to be their friends but our driving relationship was built mainly on friendly professionalism which can lose its meaning when we both go our separate ways. I also wondered what kind of friends she would have on there and whether I would end up trawling through rants and moans about who did what and to who.

After a few days I found her page and tentatively asked her to be a friend and, of course, it was immediately accepted. During the next weeks I was amazed to find she was posting the most beautiful messages about life and posts about how you should love your children because they are precious. There were the obvious cheeky and naughty posts but even they seemed to have a positive message and it reaffirmed what a shining light there was inside.

I logged onto Facebook one day and found a post from her that took me completely by surprise. It said

"Missing my midwife...doctor...teacher... therapist...advisor... FRIEND XXXX"

It is easy to judge from first impressions and believe that because somebody has lived a not so pure life, that they should be ignored as worthless. Yet, sometimes, it is the life they have led in the environment they have been brought into that shapes the soul forever, therefore these people can be better qualified to shine.

She certainly is a Diamond.

FAMILY STRIFE

Has anybody ever taught their daughter to drive? – **DON'T!** It was to be an experience that would test my professionalism and even question whether I knew what I was doing.

The first training car I had was a Nissan Micra and it was superb. As time went on it became a little tired and it was time to change if I wanted to keep the image of being the ultimate professional! So I changed the car for a Kia Rio and kept the Micra for my daughter as her first car when she passed her driving test.

When she was seventeen I offered her the chance to learn to drive and told her I would give her a discount (as if I was going to charge her but it was worth winding her up!).

She wasn't the most enthusiastic pupil but did show the necessary aptitude with the controls. However, in truth she was not ready.

Several things were not right. Firstly, she was not ready to take the responsibility of driving - it is a huge step for some people at that age. I also think she felt the pressure at school of having a Dad as an instructor and the expectation from other people that she should be able to sail through everything. She had never shown an interest in driving like other pupils do. Some people can't wait to drive, others can take it or leave it.

So her first attempts at driving were reluctant and it was a struggle to get her interested. I knew I was banging my head against a brick wall but tried to encourage her into it. She can be very stubborn at times and this came to the fore several times in no uncertain way and, as she had applied to go to University, time was running out.

Indeed she did go to University and discovered, before she went, that a car would not really be necessary there. Parking might be an issue, it costs money to run and public transport is usually pretty good around universities. And, apart from that, it seriously curtails the amount of alcohol abuse you can subject yourself to! (I was young and stupid once, remember).

So for three years she did no driving whatsoever and we used the car for storage as it sat in the garage.

After finishing her degree she reluctantly came home as jobs were scarce, and there was little chance of her finding somewhere to live that she could afford. I must admit I was devastated inside when she left for University so when she came home with the idea of using us as a temporary base I was quite glad but not so glad that all her belongings came back with her! It also meant we could carry on with the unfinished business of learning to drive.

She still wasn't that keen but managed to get a job within a couple of weeks of returning home. It was a joyous occasion not just for her but also for us as the prospect of housing an unemployed ex student was not very appealing.

The job was eight miles away and although it wasn't what she had trained for, it was interesting and it paid real money so everybody was happy. However the journey meant her getting up at ridiculous hours to walk for twenty minutes to catch a bus for a one hour journey then walk a further ten minutes to work. By car this journey would have taken twenty-five minutes from home. Of course the same journey had to be done again after a days work. Sometimes we all need a little kick up the backside to get motivated and this journey was giving her one!

So we started learning to drive again. Again, she had all the skills but was reluctant to concentrate and use them. This led to many arguments over the months with the same outcome. I would give her a telling off for making the same old mistakes and she would tell me off for shouting at her. The point I was always trying to make was that it was her who needed to take responsibility for her learning and not rely on me to keep bailing her out when things went wrong.

She had the benefit of having a Dad as a driving instructor. I blocked off a two hour lesson on her day off each week but, invariably, she would end up having a one hour lesson because she wouldn't get out of bed or she had to go somewhere (only close family would do that). When she worked at weekends she would get the chance to drive to work and back home at night. She didn't have to pay for car insurance, fuel, car tax, lessons etc.

If I asked her "What did that last road sign mean?" she would reply "For Sale!" If I asked her what is likely to be round the next bend she would say "Pandas!" Talk about banging your head against a brick wall!

Many a time I would tell her that I was stopping her driving lessons or that she should change her driving instructor and mean it. The truth is that inside I was desperately unhappy and felt like a complete failure because although I had an excellent first time pass rate and was one of the busiest driving instructors around, well liked by many, I could not even teach my own daughter.

It also caused many arguments between Ann and myself.

I had gone to collect Caitlin from her work one night and was getting fed up with her making the same mistakes and the tension in the car was tangible again. As we approached a set of crossroads I just shouted at her "assess the risk". To my surprise she slowed down and looked everywhere she needed to and dealt with the junction expertly! We approached other hazards and I just said to her "assess the risk" and she would. Suddenly for the last five minutes of the drive home she was doing everything she should!

Everybody has a different way of learning and sometimes their own way of triggering behaviour, this was obviously hers. Whenever I said this to her she would respond appropriately to the situation. Things moved on quickly from there and she seemed to develop as a person too. I always judge whether a person is ready for their driving test by watching their attitude change towards the job in hand and I was sensing just this change now in Caitlin.

On her next day off I decided to give her an assessment. This is like a mock driving test where I just give directions and take notes during the drive, in other words under test conditions. We were driving for about thirty minutes and stopped near where she needed to go for a hair appointment. While she was driving I had a really good feeling about what she was doing, she looked confident, composed, and had grown in stature as a driver. We discussed a couple of things she could have done better but I told her that if she kept up that standard then there was no reason why we shouldn't go for a driving test. "Really" she said in an excited voice. Why not?

How do I know if somebody is ready for a driving test? I follow my intuition, obviously!

She was so excited she took me to the pub and bought me lunch, she was early for her appointment and I had some time to spare before my next pupil. While we were there I felt the bond between us change. This was a confident young woman buying lunch for her Dad, a far cry from the reluctant daughter kicking and screaming at the wicked Father! While we were in the pub we were waited on by a young man I had taught to drive, we saw a friend of mine and there was generally a warm glow between us. It felt good!

I was in meditation one evening and Caitlin walked quietly into the bedroom. She asked what date to book her driving test so I asked spirit and was told February 28th. I passed this information onto her and she went away then came back a few minutes later.

"That is on a Tuesday and my day off is Thursday" I asked them again. Again they said February 28th and were quite positive about this. So Caitlin booked the test and changed her day off. This meant I had to get the Micra MOT tested, taxed and roadworthy again and, as we were trying to keep the test date a secret between ourselves, I had to do this "just in case she reached test standard in the next few months" wink, wink!

While she was getting ready to go out one night I asked her to choose an angel card. The message was "Discipline will bring freedom." Hadn't I been telling her that all this time?!

I had several messages about Caitlin from spirit during mediations leading up to her test. In one of them I saw somebody free falling uncontrollably from a plane. When I looked closer it was Caitlin. Then the parachute opened and she landed safely on earth. She immediately untied the parachute and walked away getting faster and then running. She got into a car then drove away. The message was simple, she will pass and never look back.

In another she was at the large doors of a temple wondering what to do, so she pushed them open revealing a large staircase. She was then on a throne with a crown and scepter, looking uncomfortable at being in such a lofty position. I was told that all she needs to do to open the door is to give it a push and she need not look uncomfortable with success because she will have deserved it.

The night before her test I had the best meditation of all. I saw one of my spirit guides who had picked some jasmine for her for concentration. My main Spirit guide, a Navajo Indian Chief, was looking very stern. I told him so and he said he was stern for concentration and discipline. Another of my spirit guides, a fourteen year old Navajo girl came in, jumping in the air excitedly – her gift was energy and adrenalin! My Grandma came in and said her gift was love, my Grandad came in to join her. I asked my Guardian Angel if Caitlin would have her Guardian Angel to help her the next day. "It will not be necessary, she will pass!" And with that she showed me a picture of Caitlin looking up at the spirits with great joy and achievement.

So the day came and only Caitlin and I knew about the test. Ann was decorating and we went out telling her that we had squeezed in a two hour driving lesson because she had changed her day off this week (is it wrong to tell lies?). We went to the test center, Caitlin drove off with the examiner and I felt like an expectant father! Usually I am quite relaxed at the test centre because I know the pupil can drive and it is just part of my job to get them there and get them home, but this was my daughter and this was a rite of passage that I was completely involved with.

She returned to the car park – SHE PASSED! Not only had she passed first time, she had scored hardly any faults. As the examiner walked towards me he said "I bet that's a relief!" He had no idea, or maybe he had from his own experiences!

We went home and told Ann, who had already suspected but could not believe we had kept it from her. To me it was usually just a routine part of my job but this was different. Most parents will have sent their children to an instructor for driving lessons and some of them will have given them private practice, but I had given her everything, training, private practice, fatherly advice. The struggle was worthwhile. My attitude to her had changed, I now saw a confident young woman ready to take a major step forward in life. Her attitude to me had changed – she now saw me as the professional I am. I felt I knew what I was doing again!

So my advice if your children ask you to teach them to drive?

If you want an easy life, say "No!"

If you want a challenge that will stretch the very limit of both your love and understanding of each other, and where the sense of achievement is immeasurable, say "Yes."

CHAPTER THREE

MIRROR SIGNAL MANOUVRE

MSPSLADA

The basis of all driving in the UK is the Miror-Signal-Manouvre routine, anybody who has suffered learning to drive here will tell you that. But this routine is more than just a way of passing your driving test. It is a framework with which to approach situations with the insight and knowledge you will need to be able to help you assess and decide which action is appropriate.

Whenever we make big decisions in life we stop and think before we do, or at least most of the time we do. There are situations where people have met in unusual circumstances and fallen in love, only to get married within weeks and then stay together for a very long time. But this is a rarity and is usually the result of knowing intuitively it is the right thing to do. There are more occasions where this kind of action has resulted in failure and, although I am promoting the idea of using intuition in this book, I would not want it to be confused with being impetuous! There will be a time when intuition can come firmly to the fore but that is sometimes only after careful consideration.

Over the years as a driving instructor I have used many examples and parallels to get my message across, and by resonating with a pupil on their level of understanding it is possible to make some understanding of a complicated issue. By leaving a junction too early it can be similar to making a run in football too early and being caught offside. In both cases the people did not do it deliberately but both ended up where they did not wish to be. In the case of the footballer, an offside flag and an argument with his team mates or the officials. In the case of the driver, pulling out in front of an articulated lorry!

One of the people I taught was an Indian gentleman who was in the UK on a three year contract and, whilst here, wanted to gain a UK license so he could continue to drive after the first twelve months. This is common practice for foreign nationals, just as we have the same agreement in their countries.

We had stopped during one of the lessons and he started to tell me about life back home. He had been a teacher at a University in India and was very young when he was given the post. He said that in India nobody questioned the teacher like they do in England. A teacher in India is called a guru, so I would be called a driving guru. He told me of the interview process and that all the other candidates were older and more experienced than him and therefore assumed he wouldn't get the job. He recalled how he was given the job because when they asked him why he wanted such a responsible teaching position at such a young age he told them "because I want to make a difference."

I thought that was such an inspirational thing to say at an interview. But isn't it true that we should all have the same attitude towards teaching the people around us, whether we are getting paid or not?

I have always believed that my job as a driving instructor is to make people think. A lot of teachers teach a subject, in other words they throw a subject at you in the hope you will catch it, it is how they are taught to teach it by their trainers, just like happened to me when I trained to be an instructor. But isn't it true that the teachers and the lessons you remember are the ones where the teacher made you think, making a difference to the way you remembered it?

Whenever we identify a hazard on the road it is important to plan the approach to it using the Mirror-Signal-

Position-Speed-Look-Assess-Decide-Act routine, and in the next sections I will be looking at this system. As we approach problems in our lives we can adapt this system to make some of the bigger decisions in our lives, allowing us to become more intuitive when we have all the facts to hand.

MIRRORS

Question

"Why do we look in the mirrors before taking any action?"

"Because we will fail our driving test when the examiner sees we have not!"

"Why does the examiner want us to check behind?"

"So we know what is behind"

"Why is that important?"

"So we know if there is a car behind"

"So what if there is a car behind?"

"We need to see how close it is"

"So what if it is really close?"

"I'd better make sure I don't stop suddenly otherwise it will hit me"

"But the traffic lights are on red, what are you going to do?"

"I'd better slow down early and gradually"

All I am doing is making people think. Once they start thinking they actually know the answers without me telling them. Obviously there are things that have to be taught but we are already starting to tap into their intuition (some would say common sense). So where does this mine of information come from? It is the way of knowing what is right and what feels right without necessarily knowing why.

"I'd better not stop suddenly" might be something we have discussed but, more often than not, it is just the pupil showing a knowledge that is borne out of common sense. Remember, though, we started with the pupil worried about not passing his/her driving test, nothing about their safety.

You should always act sensibly on what you see in the mirrors.

Sorry, I said mirrors as if there are lots of them. Well I suppose there are, one in the middle and two on the doors. Oh, and mirrors have blind spots as well! Contrary to popular belief, if you check your mirrors the instructions of what to do next will not magically appear like an oracle. A mirror is a piece of glass with a silver background to it so nothing mystical about that!

But what they give us is information, a reflection of what is behind, how close and how fast, also if the traffic behind is changing position.

So here is the scenario. You can hear a motorbike behind just as you are about to turn across the traffic into a turning on the opposite side of the road. You have checked your centre mirror and your door mirror but can't see the motorbike. It is ok to turn isn't it?

No. What if the motorbike is just about to overtake you but is hidden in a blind spot as you look? If you look in the other door mirror he may be visible which means he is safely out of your way. If you check over your shoulder you may see him on your tail waiting patiently for you to turn before he also turns behind you. If you can't see him it does not mean he is not there so the phrase we use is "effective observation", in other words use whatever means you can to make sure you are not going to harm him before you turn.

What we are in effect doing is being aware of our surroundings, picking up where everybody is and what has changed. When we look behind us in our lives we can see where we have been and what we have done but things change, sometimes quickly. If we are not aware of our surroundings we cannot hope to know at what point we are at in our lives.

When we look in the mirror it is too easy to start regretting things like "I wish I hadn't taken that corner so wide" The truth is, as bad as it was, we survived and we have learnt not to do it again. We may have done it because we approached too fast – another lesson. Learning the lesson is good but if we dwell on it too long we may forget what we are trying to do at that moment, like turning.

But life is the same. When asked "Have you any regrets?" most of us say the same thing "Too many to mention!"

But are they regrets or are they lessons we have learnt which have made us better at what we do? Without making mistakes there would be no improvement. I am not suggesting anybody puts anybody in danger and tries to make deliberate errors because we all make mistakes anyway, then you can go through this process.

But, as I suggested with effective observation, are we just checking the mirrors we were told to check or are we using effective observation. In other words are we getting the bigger picture? How many times do we do something then say, "If I'd known you were there I wouldn't have done that!" So I suppose the question is why didn't you look first, then you would have been aware of who was there.

The truth is we are usually too occupied living our hectic lives to be concerned about the bigger picture so we end up doing the least amount of work possible to achieve what we believe is a good option! When it goes wrong we kick ourselves and ask ourselves why we didn't just look that little bit harder.

So what is the bigger picture?

In a car, it is looking at the effect of our driving on other road users. For example, if I see in the rear view mirror an ambulance approaching with its blue lights flashing do

I continue to block the road, waiting to turn, knowing I will hold it up, or do I pull over until it has gone and then approach the turn?

If I hold it up will it mean the patient it is trying to get to will lose their life because of the holdup?

If I pull up will that cause a blockage that will mean the ambulance can't get through anyway?

Would it be better to drive past the turn and drive to the wider part of the road I can see ahead where the ambulance can get safely past? I can always find a different route afterwards.

But if we do not see the bigger picture in the first place it is easy to panic when the siren suddenly sounds over the volume of the radio and we end up making a mess and getting in the way because we were only aware of our direct surroundings, not the bigger picture.

Do you think the car that is too close behind is that close because he is totally unaware of the bigger picture, for example, we might have to stop suddenly if the green traffic light ahead changes. I have lost count of the times my inexperienced pupil has panicked and then said, "I feel like just slamming the brake on and teaching him". Drivers beware!

Life is like that. We are all guilty of saying things like "Oh, if only I'd realized", "Do you know, it never occurred to me until you said." The problem is we need to see the bigger picture to understand where our actions fit, only then can we begin to plan our actions better.

SIGNALS

So now we have information, how do we use it?

Signals are for the benefit of other people, not for us or the examiner. The examiner will not be impressed if you wind the window down and show him the slowing down arm signal every time you approach traffic lights! What will impress him is using an appropriate signal in the appropriate situations at the appropriate time. Generally, early enough so other road users can make their plans.

It is no good telling a following driver you are going to turn left as you are actually turning left, the manouvre itself is making it clear but the following driver may ask "Why didn't you tell me you were going to turn left, I would have given you more room and you wouldn't have taken me by surprise."

It is also no good putting on an indicator for the turn on your near side before you go past the van that is parked on the same side before the turn. This makes it look like you are parking before reaching the van and causes confusion when you then move out and go round the van, opposite to what you signaled. Again the response might be "I didn't expect you to move around the van as I started to go past you"

I am keeping these responses pleasant and reasonable but, as we all know, today's roads are not the most forgiving and tolerant places around!

So how do we know how and when to signal?

The Highway Code presents us with the available signals and all we have to do is choose which one. Simple!

Indicators are the ones everybody thinks of when signals are mentioned, as if it is the only signal we have to worry about. True, it is an important one because it tells other people which direction we intend to move, left or right. Notice I said "intend" - a signal is only an intention and does not give us the obligation to do it. As a Motorcycle instructor friend of mine says to his pupils "All an indicator means is that the bulb is working."

So if we are turning left or right we need an indicator - but what about the timing? We need to do it early and clearly so everybody knows we will be slowing down and making the turn. But if we do it too early people might get confused, certainly if we signal before the first road on the left or right when we are actually going to take the second one!

So we need to see the bigger picture first, before we signal – cue mirrors and effective observation.

It is amazing to this day how many people still indicate before going round a parked car just because their instructor told them to do it! What if there is a road on the opposite side, might it look like we are waiting behind the parked car because we are intending to turn into the side road? This bigger picture is getting bigger and bigger!

So what other signals are available?

Brake lights warn following road users we are braking and slowing down, possibly coming to a stop. Many learners have a habit of putting the handbrake on before the car has stopped, a habit which is discouraged pretty quickly. Apart from the sudden stop and wear to the car, the handbrake does not bring on the brake lights so it is unfair to the driver behind who sees us stop suddenly in front of him without warning. And, let's be honest, how many times do we see the car behind only slow down when they see our brake lights, it wakes them up?!

Reverse lights warn we are intending to reverse, other road users then know to keep a clear space behind us assuming the signal is early enough or the following driver is seeing the bigger picture.

Arm signals (not hand signals!) are in the Highway code and can be used if any lights are not working or if they are needed to back up a signal already being used.

Along with flashing headlamps and sounding the horn, the general public has devised its own set of rules for communicating with other road users. Flashing headlamps are now used for various reasons, "I'll let you out", "Thanks", "There is a police speed camera round this bend", "Hello, mate" are examples. The problem is that if somebody flashes their headlamps, it is sometimes difficult to know why they are flashing. But the dangerous thing about flashing headlamps is that it puts pressure on the other driver to react in some way.

We are all human so our first reaction is to try and do something without holding up the nice person who has flashed us. This then leads to rushing out of a junction, or crossing the road without looking in an attempt to show we are grateful to this nice person (who is trying to kill us!). And the crazy thing is that if we don't go the nice person then drives past shaking their head as if we were stupid for taking the time to make sure it was safe!

Nobody doubts the good intentions of this action but it could have been safer. Never invite a person who is in a safe place into one where they could be in danger. Leave a space open and make eye contact and smile but let the other person decide once they have assessed the risk, it is their life after all! And quite often the flashing headlamp is unnecessary anyway. We have all been guilty of flashing our headlamps on a bright sunny day. We have all stopped to let a car out of a junction then realized there was nothing behind us and the other driver was just waiting for us to go past and now confusion reigns!

So the signals we send out sometimes have an impact on traffic without us realizing the effect.

If we position the car appropriately then this can act as a very strong signal. Returning to going around a parked car, do we need an indicator if it is a clear day and your position makes it obvious what you are doing, (you can tell by the way traffic behind is following you in a sensible way or not)?

If we approach at a positive speed does it not send out a signal to other road users of our intention to keep moving? We should always be able to stop safely in the distance we can see clear ahead, but if we slow down too early that can encourage people to take advantage of a situation that they felt unable to take before.

So the signals we send out when we are driving are sometimes unintentional but what about the signals we, ourselves, give out to other people?

If we are in an office we have the advantage of being able to talk to people to tell them our intentions like "I'm just going to the toilet".

We can phone people or text them with our intentions like "I'm just going to the shop on the way home so I'll be a bit late".

What about the signals that are sent without realizing it? How is it that we get a feeling one of our colleagues isn't quite themselves today? We can't put our finger on it but something doesn't quite feel right. Where does this feeling come from?

Call it intuition.

Without getting too deep we can attribute a lot to our auric field. We all have an aura around us which is an energy field made up of several chakras. This field expands and contracts and changes colour to match how we are feeling. As our field changes so do those of others and as they meet they send out and pick up signals to and from each other. So if a colleague is having a troubled time this will affect their aura and, without realizing it, your aura will pick up this sensitive energy change.

This then leads to the question "What signals are you sending out?" Are they positive, tired, determined, sad, happy?

What about when you are challenged by a colleague when they ask "You don't seem yourself today, is anything wrong?"

We are all the same and we will reply "No, I'm fine, just a little tired" or "It's nothing, just a bit stressed with moving house." We pass it off when really we know we have been rumbled! And your colleagues then give you a wide berth for the rest of the day because they do not know what to say or do! That is when your friends can help because it is they who will demand to know what is wrong and usually have a plan of how to ease it.

The opposite happens too when people ask "Have you won the lottery, you are very chirpy?"

I have taken lots of pupils back to their parents after passing their driving test and, despite their best and convincing efforts to tell them they failed, their parents know they have passed – how do they do that?

Try this one when next in a shop. I was brought up in the golden era of vinyl records, a product that was exciting and tactile, the artwork was usually a masterpiece which could be appreciated for all it's glory on a 12" LP Cover. The words were large enough to read and the photos on the cover gave a wonderful insight into way the band looked! Call me old fashioned but buying a CD is not the same, and as for downloads! I digress but there was a strange phenomenon that happened in a record shop and it still happens today. My favourite rock band is Rush, and if I wanted to check out which albums of theirs I hadn't got yet there would always be somebody there checking out all the "Ns, Os, Ps, Qs, Rs, Ss", and so on. As LPs were 12" wide it was difficult to see and the other person would be flipping the LP's one at a time. What I noticed was that if I stood next to them and started checking out the rack next to them a strange thing would happen. I was obviously sending out the signal "I want to look at what you're looking at" unintentionally. They would receive the message subconsciously and move on without finishing the rack they were looking at! I had not put pressure on, they had not acknowledged me being there but somehow the signal had been sent and received without even looking at each other! I am not an expert in telepathy and certainly did not know what I know now about psychic "stuff" but it was a useful skill. Likewise, I always seemed to know when I was being pressured to move out of the way so somebody else could come and have a browse. It is easy to pass this off as body language but isn't that the very thing we are discovering? The signal we send out from our aura and inner self is received sometimes as body language, sometimes just a feeling or an intuition.

As I am a man I am going to ask the next question from a man's perspective, girls can play along too.

A young attractive female walks into the room and you immediately fall in love with this woman (love as in WOW, not unconditional love, not at first sight!). You can't take your eyes off her and you don't know what it is that you like about her but she has totally captured you. As the minutes go by you start to notice things wrong with her. She has a slightly crooked nose. Her hair colour is not your usual preference. She is taller than you normally like. Her skin is not perfect. Her legs are a bit fat. I could continue picking on this poor woman but you get the picture. In other words, when you study her, there are definite things about her that you would not like in your ideal woman. But the overall effect is stunning and you don't know why, in fact you don't care about the bad bits! So do you fancy the woman who has just walked into the room or do you fancy the spirit that has entered in all its complete and radiant beauty?

Where does the signal of beauty come from, the physical or the spiritual? And how is that signal interpreted by those receiving it, physically or spiritually? Your intuition will know.

So, as far as signals go, if we are sending out the wrong signals then people are going to get the wrong message. Likewise, if we are unable to read the signals of others we are going to misunderstand them and act wrongly to them.

Some signals we can change, it is up to us to make sure we realize this. Those we cannot are down to our inner self but I can assure you, the most positive signals you will find in life are those sent out by your intuition. Once you are in tune with it, the signals are clear and strong and shouldn't be doubted.

POSITION

So, what position are we in at the moment?

Position is an important part of driving: it shows other people where we are, it keeps us away from danger and we can position ourselves to secure a good view.

Normal road position when driving a car is one metre from the kerb on a normal width road.

This is the industry standard and is because it leaves a safe clearance from the kerb and keeps you out of the rubbish and potholes at the side. It also leaves room for error if you lose steering control or if you need to move over a bit for a wide vehicle, as well as sending out a strong signal that you are moving and not kerb crawling, as discussed in the last section. So that's ok then.

I have taught pupils who have come to me and told me that they struggle to keep a metre from the kerb and have had several lessons where their instructor has spent all that time trying to get them to drive exactly at this distance. What a waste of time, and by the end of this section you will see why.

Remember the bigger picture? There are several reasons why this industry standard position may not be suitable.

If the road is narrow you may have to drive closer to the kerb to leave enough room for vehicles coming towards you to get past, whilst also making sure you do not get too close to the kerb.

If there is an obstruction ahead like a parked car then we will have to change our position so we do not drive into the back of it!

If we intend to overtake an articulated lorry or other large vehicle we may have to move closer to the centre of the road so we can see the road past the lorry, otherwise we will never know if it is safe to overtake. Every day I see car drivers starting to overtake from a position where they couldn't see and were totally oblivious to the danger they are now accelerating towards – sometimes us!

So what is the point of religiously following a line a metre from the kerb? All it encourages us to do is look to the side to see where the kerb is. Surely the skill is to look as far ahead as you can and get **THE BIGGER PICTURE!**

Only then will you see where to position the car. If there are no obstructions and the road is clear then a metre from the kerb is ideal but nobody is going to get a tape measure out and check it. By looking well ahead the eyes are sending signals to the brain to tell it where they want you to direct the car. If the car is moving towards the kerb the eyes will pick this up and send a message to move away. Likewise if the car starts to move to the centre the eyes will again remind the brain where they want to go and the brain will send the signals to come back over a little.

The other main reason is that if there is anything ahead that warrants a change of position, a parked car for instance, this early warning can be used to start planning a line to take around the obstruction, leaving space around it for safety and then moving back into a normal position for the rest of the road.

Within a couple of lessons these new pupils would have cured their fear of kerbs and also would now be planning a route for themselves, in other words they were now planning and using their own common sense/ intuition to know where the best position for the car would be, regardless of what the text books had told them.

So already we have empowered a novice to use his or her intuition to know where the car should be but we will come across situations which need a lot more thought about where to put the car. Sometimes the question has to be "Where do you NOT want to put the car?" This is sometimes easier to answer, for example, "Not in the ditch" or "not on the wrong side of the road". Now we have ruled out where we do not want to be, we can look at the rest of the options available to us.

What if we cannot see what we need to see to make a good decision? We may have to move the car to a place where the view is better. This is true when we are creeping and peeping from a side road.

A simple question is all I need to get the point across "as a pedestrian would you cross the road with a blindfold on?" The answer is always the same "No that would be stupid!"

So why do we try and pull out from a side road without being able to see if it is safe first? Surely the safest thing to do is to improve the view carefully until we can see what we need to see to make a good decision. So our viewing position is important.

If we have to change our position then it is important we plan the change for everybody's safety and convenience – bring back mirrors, then necessary signals, correctly timed.

Position is also a positive way of being assertive as long as we do not use it aggressively or without consideration for others. It is sometimes necessary to get an early road position in order to block the path of other vehicles and stop them trying to use space that is not rightfully theirs.

Let me explain this for the UK roads.

You want to turn right at the roundabout ahead so you check your mirrors and see a car speeding up behind you that looks like it also wants to turn right. An early signal is essential but so too is an early position. Once you have that position the traffic now has to follow you safely from behind because you have closed the door to his possible overtake. If you do not get that early position it then allows him to overtake, leaving you in a vulnerable position and not able to get to the correct position safely. It makes you more likely to panic, confuses other traffic, and may hold up the whole traffic system as you battle to get into the correct position when you could have been there well before the following car made his move. We should never move carelessly in front of other traffic but getting a good early position puts us in control and sets us up nicely to assess what we need to do next.

The human brain sees space as something it needs to fill. How many times have you looked at a room in the house and decided you need some furniture to fill that empty space in the corner?

If you leave a gap long enough on the road, somebody will fill it. When leaving a roundabout from a right turn it is essential to close the door on the left by moving to the left lane as soon as possible after the last exit before yours. If you don't, then you are leaving open the possibility of somebody filling it because they have seen the space but not the bigger picture!

I usually draw two doors on a piece of paper then, depending who I am teaching, I tell the pupil they are on holiday. "Here are two night clubs next door to each other. They both have the same opening hours, same drinks, same prices, same music, everything about them is exactly the same." Then I draw a stick figure in one of them and tell them there is a bouncer stood in the doorway of one of them.

Which one do you enter?

More often than not they would go into the empty one because it was an open space with no resistance. Occasionally somebody would say the one with the bouncer because the riff-raff would be in the other one! But this proves the point even more; if you leave a door open the riff-raff will use it without thinking - there is no deterrent. So getting a good early positive position is a way of keeping the riff-raff out – sorry I mean stopping people from inadvertently using the space you want without thinking!

If I was teaching a footballer I would tell them the ball is over there and an opponent is over here. How do you stop him getting to the ball without fouling him? Easy – stand in between the player and the ball, now he has to go round you!

So back to the original question, what position are we in at the moment?

As we have seen from driving, position is very important and, although we have a normal idea of what it should be, it is necessary for the position to change several times during a journey as the situations around us change.

If we do not look at the bigger picture then we really do not know where we are, are we near the kerb or are we about to meet impending doom by driving into the back of an obstruction?

My position has changed several times over the years, or at least my perception of where I thought I was has changed. Little did I think, all those years ago whilst working in the Motor Trade, that one day I would be writing a book.

In fact, two and a half years ago I was just merrily teaching people to drive, totally unaware of the changes about to hit me in my life. The strange fact is that these changes have made me aware of what my actual position is. Before I saw the bigger picture I was just a learner in life trying to hug the kerb for dear life because that is what I was told I had to do!

As my journey into spirituality sped along I was drawn into the crazy time that was 2012 and the Cosmic Moment of December 21st. Many people knew it as the end of the world, a message that was spread by Armageddon enthusiasts and misguided media outlets. The truth was that the Mayan long count calendar was coming to an end (other calendars were coming to an end too) and the planets and stars would align in a way seen very rarely in the history of the Universe. This would release massive energy towards the earth that would help her to ascend to a higher consciousness that we would all benefit from.

But to accept this energy, things had to be prepared. The earth is a generally negative place so great areas of the earth were cleansed and re-energized with wind and rain causing floods in many areas. In other words, the earth was making sure it was in the correct position to accept this energy.

Also, there was a quickening change in society and in people to position them for this change. Have you ever thought it strange that the world economies seemed to be collapsing en masse and that there seemed to be a deluge of scandal stories involving celebrities as the truth was finally being revealed about their hidden pasts?

Have you wondered about the sudden influx of comets, fireballs and sonic booms around the world, all of which NASA and Governments could not explain, most of which never got reported by the media?

Have you thought about how many relationships you knew that split up in the run up to December 2012?

All of these things were happening as the earth and its inhabitants were being put into the correct position ready for the new energy.

Ask yourself honestly, what was life like before Christmas 2012 and what it is like now?

If you are like me, you may feel that you are in a better position to meet the future than you have ever been and look back in amazement at the chaos that reigned in 2012 as we were all being put exactly where we needed to be.

So position is vitally important and, although it may be difficult for us to understand, we have been placed in a position to enable us to see the bigger picture and change it whenever we see an obstruction that is holding us back.

SPEED

You should always be able to stop in the distance that is safe ahead.

If there is a major complaint about most drivers today it is that they drive too fast and too close. If something happens ahead there is little room for error. When a pile-up happens on a motorway involving several cars there is always an outpouring of sympathy, quite rightly, for those who have been killed or seriously injured, and for their families too.

I am going to play devil's advocate now but suppose there are thirty-two cars in a pile up. The first car may well have been caught by surprise by a freak incident and not been able to stop in time. This may have caught out the second car driver also, but the other thirty drivers? If they had all kept a safe distance from the vehicle in front then wouldn't they all have been able to stop and go to the help of the first driver and their occupants?

When we talk about speed in driving, people always assume that as long as they are under the speed limit they are safe but a speed limit is only a legal requirement. What we should determine is an appropriate speed.

So how do we know what is appropriate?

When I was being trained to be a driving instructor I was told how to train somebody about speed approaching a junction. The pupil was told to get their speed down to walking pace three car lengths before the junction. Easy!

First of all what is walking pace? I suppose it is four miles per hour for the average human being, but how can you explain this to the poor student? If their eyes are glued to the speedometer we lose sight of where we are on the road and other controls get forgotten. The best description I once saw was in a magazine article that read, "If it feels too slow then that's walking pace!" At last, something you can feel – remember intuition?

All we need to do now is to figure out what is three car lengths. The Highway Code suggests that the average car length is four metres long so three car lengths equals twelve metres. Bingo! Then the pupil says "I'm rubbish with metres, what is that in feet?"

"Fifteen?"

"How far is that?"

So we are non the wiser.

To determine what is a good speed it is important to understand why we are slowing down because, contrary to popular belief, we are not slowing down because your instructor told you to do so! We have a lot of work to do approaching any junction before we can safely turn. These things will be covered in more detail in the next sections but when you have read them you may find this part on speed a good place to return to and read again.

We have to think about what we are doing. I will cover the way we look, assess, decide and act shortly but we also have to prepare ourselves and the car for what we are going to do. In other words, it is important that we have enough time to plan and prepare.

We have to select the correct gear. Gears are not black and white and there is no set formula for which gear to be in despite what some sources might say. I have had pupils who say their last instructor told them it was second gear for a left turn, first for a right. So this explains why they are selecting second gear when they are clearly going to have to stop because the road is blocked. Also, why they are selecting first gear for a turn when they can see clearly that they can just continue driving smoothly into it in second gear. The truth is that gears are intuitive. If it feels right it is right. As long as the car feels under control and there is enough power in the gear to accelerate out of trouble if needed, then does it matter what gear number it is?

Gears take up most pupils' thought process most of the time, as do the other controls in the early stages of learning. It is understandable. As much as I may be pointing out what they should be looking for on the road, I can tell in the early stages that all they are thinking is "How do I stop this car and how do I start it again?" But that will not stop me pointing out hazards as it is this skill that is essential. Car control is important but it is no good explaining to the Judge that, "I crashed into the tree because I didn't see it but I was in the correct gear for the speed!" If you see the tree in plenty of time, the car can now be controlled in an appropriate way to avoid the hazard safely – not the other way round!

So the battle with gears is to make the pupil understand that speed is important, not the gears. If we slow down in plenty of time we will then have enough time to plan and change gear safely, thus preparing the car for what we are about to do next.

So speed becomes an important part of creating time to plan and prepare (I know it is against the scientific laws of Physics to create time but that is the illusion. And anyway, time is a man made creation to try and put things in order; time does not exist in the spirit world.) So gears are based on their feeling, if it feels right it is right, if it doesn't then it needs to change – use your intuition!

So we can have scientific ways of calculating approach speed and when to slow down but I found a better way of doing it that will make sense after we have discussed how to look and assess so bear with me and feel free to re-read this section on speed at a later time. As we approached a junction I would tell them to kill their speed. If they didn't do it early enough I would tell them to do it earlier. If they didn't get the speed down to a slow enough speed I would tell them to kill the speed right down almost to a stop. If there was still a problem I would tell them to stop, usually about ten metres from the junction (obviously when nobody was behind). I would then tell them to go into first gear and slowly manouvre up to the junction and negotiate the junction as they thought was necessary. When they had done this, usually quite well, I would ask them "How much time did you have then?" They would admit they had enough time to control the car, make sure it was safe, keep their position, change their mind, point out the flowers in the gardens and all without holding anybody up! The point was made – an appropriate speed should give us time to think about what we are going to do so that we make the best decisions and are fully prepared to carry them out. Obviously people think and do at different speeds, so some would slow down earlier than others, some would be able to think quicker so would leave the slowing down a little bit later, but what we had achieved was a speed appropriate for that person to be able to plan and prepare properly.

So how much time do we make for ourselves when we need to plan and prepare? Be honest!

Isn't it the same every Christmas when we all say "I'm not ready for Christmas, it's suddenly crept up on me." No it hasn't! It happens on the same date every year, as one Christmas finishes we have a full twelve months to prepare for the next one! I am smiling because I fall into the same trap. So how is something as obvious and predictable as Christmas missed? Could it be the speed at which we live our lives?

I don't know about you but there have been times in my life when I have just eaten, slept, worked and had no time for anything other than just breathing! I can look back now and criticize myself for being so stupid but the fact is we all have to live. We have children to look after and ferry around. We have jobs to go to, some of those jobs with very high demands, I know that from experience. We fill our spare time with hobbies and societies, laughingly calling them leisure.

So where do you make the time to think? In the bath? In bed? Having a cup of tea? On the bus?

It doesn't matter where we do it, the important thing is that we make time for it. I have spoken about meditation before and it is not an art for the privileged or the lazy, we can all do it, even if it just means making a cup of tea and chilling for half an hour.

Research in America has discovered that those of us who daydream are better able to work out complicated issues than those who go rushing round all day looking important. The funny thing is that those people who are busily rushing around all day looking important usually spend most of the day telling people they are important and can't stop, "I haven't got time to stop, I've got important things to do." Is it any wonder these are the people who are unfulfilled in life and quite often end up in an early grave or on tablets for the rest of their lives, having alienated most of the people they have come into contact with?

So speed is appropriate. When the time is right, by all means make progress, do the things at the speed required to get the job done. But when complications appear, make enough time to deal with them properly otherwise they will be unplanned and you will be unprepared for them.

But most of all, live your life at a speed where there is always time for contemplation, this will take you back to your inner self and your intuition. It is there you will find the answers to your problems and the feelings that are missed when you drive past too quickly.

LOOK

Look for information.

That sounds simple enough but how often are we guilty of looking but not seeing? There are things around us that do not or will not change.

In driving terms this could mean the road layout, the road markings, whose priority is it? Do we have to give way or stop? How much can we see, is there a fixed blind spot like a bend or brow of a hill for example?

Most of this information can be visible from distance so we can already start to plan things such as position; where do we need to put the car for the direction we are heading?

Is there something unusual we need to investigate further as we get nearer? We might have approached situations like this many times but this particular one is slightly different and means we have to think about what we might have to do slightly differently.

We talked about speed in the previous section as a way of creating time to think but here the skill is looking for the information early, in other words, if we start to get the information as soon as we can we will have plenty of time to work out a good plan. If we think we can wait until we get closer to it we may end up getting too close and running out of time then being caught out by the information that was actually quite obvious if only we had looked for it straight away.

I refer back to Christmas. As we start the New Year we already have the information about what dates next Christmas will be and we know exactly what format it will take. We have done it several times before but we always ignore the information, believing it is not important at this time as, quite rightly, there are other more important things to think about. But we keep on leaving it until we look up and suddenly it is the week before Christmas! Yet we had all the information last year! In fact we know the dates of Christmas for the next foreseeable number of years!

This is how most of us live our lives. We never actually see the information because we believe it is not relevant at the moment, when actually there is always relevance in what we see. We walk around our towns and cities with our heads down, only digesting the information we believe is important to us.

In my birthplace of Manchester you are always advised to look up at the buildings when you walk around. Most people only look as high as eye level. If you do this you will see what the city has become - shops, businesses, hotels, etc. But if you look up you will see the glorious past of a great City. I am biased, of course, because Manchester is my birthplace but do the same thing in any city and you will see the most amazing buildings giving you an insight into the heritage of the place you are in.

My brother used to walk past Big Ben every day when he worked in London, then one day looked up as he went past and suddenly realized it was Big Ben!

Why is it that we only become concerned about our heritage when somebody wants to remove it? We look at the fields surrounding our towns without a second thought yet when a developer wants to build on them we suddenly become protective because we have realized the beauty of the area and how lucky we are to live in an a place that gives us so much pleasure.

It is a clear example of looking but not seeing.

As an exercise, when you are in your garden or local park, just choose one of the flowers you are near to.

Do not pick it unless you own it and always ask the flowers permission first - it will willingly agree if you ask from the heart. Then study it. Do not try and work out the cell structure or the chemicals involved, let the scientists do that. But look at the colours, the shapes, the patterns. Lose yourself in the beauty of that flower and let your inner self make a connection with it. I guarantee that you will see it from a completely different perspective than when just glanced at from a distance.

Then, as you look at it, ask your inner self to come forward and give you some wisdom from the flower. Do not search for something earth shattering, just listen for the simplest thought you have because, just for that moment, you are at one with that flower.

The truth is we are at one with every living thing and the Universe, we are all one of the same creation but we all have different roles to play.

So if we are guilty of anything, it is that, quite often, we look but do not really see.

ASSESS

Things change all the time and need to be assessed constantly.

When I use the word "assess" in driving it usually means weighing up the options, looking for opportunities and realizing the risks.

If we use a junction as an example we can begin to think about what is likely to change and what options are open to us.

In the last section we talked about looking for information and how we were concerned with things that would not change, in other words, it would still be a T-junction, it would still be a give way junction, we still wouldn't be able to see when we got there.

This section is looking at the variables, the things that are likely to change as we approach.

Pedestrians. They are the most vulnerable road users we will meet. They always have priority on the road, even if they don't deserve it, because they will be hurt the most in a collision. When I say they don't deserve it, of course I mean the times when they cross the road without looking. For example, Mobile phones are a Godsend these days but have also become a distraction in our daily lives. I have lost count of the times I have seen people walk across a road without looking whilst their phone is glued to their ear. We all do it, though - I have probably done it myself.

Cyclists and motor cyclists. We all know about the dangers, we are reminded all the time, but there is still a feeling amongst car drivers that cyclists are a nuisance and are always getting in the way. They have every right to use the roads but they are easily hidden and can seem to appear from nowhere making them extremely vulnerable. It is true that there are bad cyclists and motorcyclists, but isn't that true of any group of people?

Other car drivers. Yes, there are bad car drivers too and we hear people moan all the time about the poor standard of driving on our roads and the "You'll never guess what somebody did to me today…." stories!

Blind spots. These can be caused by the road layout such as a bad bend or a large building. I hear you say "but a building will not change so it is in the wrong section." True, the building will not change but the traffic will change around it, in other words we have to allow for the change in traffic.

So why are they so variable?

The main problem is that we have several human beings all trying to assess the situation from their own perspective and trying to make their own decisions. Enter human error!

We are all only human after all. I know we are spiritual beings in a physical body but we have been given free will to mess it up and try and get it right!

We all have differing ability to judge speed and distance. A young child, for instance, has not developed a feeling for speed yet and is likely to cross the road whereas a middle-aged person would not. An elderly person with deteriorating eyesight might misjudge distance where they would have accurately assessed it in younger times.

An inexperienced driver will still be getting used to judging speed of vehicles at junctions and will get it wrong occasionally.

The funny thing is that we all know when we get it wrong but the reaction of the other driver is quite often the same "Look at that idiot". But the person isn't an idiot at all, they just got it wrong and are probably driving away wishing they could talk to the other driver and apologize. When we bump into each other in the street we apologize immediately and the other party often also apologizes. In a car we rarely get the chance to say sorry, so we are left with this cloud hanging over us that somebody has dared to misjudge a situation and it being made worse by the reaction of the victim.

They may have been driving all day and made hundreds of perfectly safe decisions but on this occasion they just got it wrong (human error).

They may be feeling unwell and are actually trying to get home to safety but their judgement is temporarily affected.

They may be driving an unfamiliar car that is not as responsive as their own and didn't pull away as fast as they thought it would.

So there are many reasons why we get it wrong, most of them down to human error or mis-judgement.

I always teach my pupils to make eye contact with the other road user. This gives a valuable insight into what they are thinking and also makes it a human contact. Now they can sort it out between themselves.

The eyes are the windows of the soul and should not be under estimated. Quite often, when eye contact is made, it becomes apparent that the other driver is a respectable looking person who is smiling and quite happy for you to go first.

So what are we afraid of, why do we not trust the other people on the road? Bad experience maybe, or the fear of seeing something in the other person we did not want to see? But if we made eye contact we would see this in their eyes before they did it. How do I know this?

Intuition! It is the feeling that you know what is going to happen next, then saying smugly to yourself "I knew he or she was going to do that!"

The roads are probably one of the most intolerant places in the modern world. Everybody seems to assume too much and not actually think about the decision the other person is trying to make.

But isn't that true of life in general? Aren't we quick to judge others before we have assessed the situation and got the full facts?

If a person was bitten by a dog in their childhood, isn't it reasonable to expect them to be at least wary around dogs? But how many times do we hear of people saying about their dogs "Don't be silly, he won't bite, just stay still". Try convincing the poor victim of that.

Is it wrong for somebody to be a quiet person who is more comfortable in his own company? Then why do we assume something is wrong and insist they go to the doctor because "they are not right".

Is it wrong for somebody to say they believe in God? It attracts all the negative feelings of people who are opposed to religions without finding out what that person's definition of God is!

So we can be judgemental without knowing the facts and as a result we become intolerant.

Had we assessed the child who was bitten by a dog we would understand their fear and keep our dog at a safe distance.

If we assessed the quiet person and understood why they were happy, we would be tolerant enough to leave them alone.

If we understood what events led to a person believing in God, we would tolerate their view even if it was not our own.

To make a decision we need to have assessed ALL the facts and not just from our own angle. There may be something we cannot see that makes another person do or say something that took us by surprise. If we had seen what they had seen, then we would probably have made the same judgement but without that knowledge we cannot judge them on the decisions they make.

Judging a person does not define who they are – it defines who you are

DECIDE

How do we make a decision? Do we make a decision then change our minds? Do we make a decision without thinking then get it wrong?

When I'm teaching driving there is a process we perform to get to this point, the process I have described so far in this chapter. When we have looked and assessed the options, we will have the information we need to make a decision.

In driving, the decisions can be made simpler. If we are turning into the traffic flow, for example, we must be able to carry on without making other traffic change speed or direction unnecessarily. If we are crossing the traffic to turn, we must be able to do the same but we must also be able to cross the path of the oncoming traffic without making it change either speed or direction. We also need to make sure we have a clear exit and make progress at an appropriate speed for the new road.

It sounds simple but there is a high degree of judgement involved. If a car is a good distance away and traveling at a modest speed, then that should give us plenty of time to make the turn and speed up. If a car is quite close and traveling at a good pace then it would be foolish to pull out in front of it.

But there is a huge middle ground where a vehicle may be a good distance away but traveling very fast. Also, a car might be really close to us but traveling so slowly that there is plenty of time to go.

So how do we come to a decision?

How many times have you been in a car with a driver who says of another driver "They had loads of time to go then". The other driver obviously didn't think so, so what made the two people think differently?

The most difficult part of teaching people to drive is to teach judgement. It does improve with practise because, like anything, the more you do it the more comfortable you feel at judging situations. In the early days I can use examples and phrases like "If, as a pedestrian, you would be able to walk across the road without making the oncoming traffic slow down or have to swerve, then as long as you have prepared the car you have got time to drive across". But we don't have time to over deliberate and calculate things because then it is seen as hesitant and holding people up, so how do we decide?

Many, many times I am asked by a pupil "Should I go?". It would be so easy for me to say yes or no but I don't, I always ask "What do you think?" I imagine you are all thinking that this is a dangerous game to play and my Guardian Angel must be quaking at the thought of having to rescue me from another fine mess, but the pupil mostly makes a good decision. The ball has been thrown back into their court and they have been forced to make a decision based on how they feel. If they misjudge it and are a little too eager I can always stop them with the dual controls if they do not respond to my screams of "stop!" If they are a bit over cautious they usually realize and tell me they could have gone after all. But nobody has been hurt. The only thing is that we may have held up the traffic behind for a little longer than needed. I do have a sign on the back of my car requesting "Please be patient" and most people are.

Imagine their surprise in a difficult situation when they ask me "What should I do here?" and I respond by saying to them "You sort it out." I am not being irresponsible or cruel, what I am doing is empowering them to think

146

for themselves and work out the answer to a complicated situation. If I feel they are struggling I will advise them a little but I do not tell them what to do. When the crisis has passed and we are safely parked I will explain that I didn't actually teach them what to do, all I did was advise or offer a target for them to reach that they reached themselves.

Obviously there will have been training to get to this standard, but this is my way of transferring the responsibility to them, I am letting them think for themselves and as a result they begin to use their own intuition to work things out. How do I know it is intuition they are using? I ask them how it felt?

The answer, when it worked well, is "It felt fine, I knew it was right and didn't see any reason why I shouldn't do it"

The answer, when it didn't work out, is "That felt awful, I just didn't feel comfortable and I knew it was the wrong thing to do as soon as I started to do it"

So one has a good feeling while the other does not feel right at all. How do I know if they are ready for a driving test? It is when they make decisions that feel right and I get a good feeling that their decisions feel good.

At last we have reached the point at which our intuition is guiding us. Without the necessary information it is difficult to decide but with the information, our intuition can come and help us.

When we buy a television we do not just turn up at the TV shop and buy the first one we see, although some people possibly do! We look at what's on offer, we assess the attributes of each television and whether it is what we need or don't need as well as the price. Then, armed with that information, we decide which one is best for us. How many times do we get a feeling for one product over the other, even though they may offer similar features? Put it another way, how often do we buy a product and then regret it saying that we should have bought the other one? This is a result of going against our intuition!

We all hear of a woman's intuition but let me cause chaos by giving you this example. I am going to generalize but bear with me.

A man goes shopping for a jacket. He goes into a clothes shop and is drawn to a particular jacket on a rail. He tries it on and buys it. Job done in five minutes, only for his wife to say, "You only bought that so we could go home!"

A woman goes shopping for a jacket. She goes into a clothes shop and is drawn to a particular jacket on a rail. She tries it on and loves it but then proceeds to try on every other jacket in the shop, taking twenty minutes to do so, before trying the first jacket on again and buying it.

This may sound familiar but if you analyze it they have both used their intuition to make the purchase. The man immediately knew it was right for him. So did the woman but she challenged her intuition by trying the other jackets on, then gave in to intuition in the end. So is a woman's intuition better than a man's? In this example no, they are both the same, but what it shows is that we are prepared to ignore our intuition in favour of something we believe to be better. I will admit there are times when I have felt the urge to get the shopping done quickly, usually when there is a game of football involved!

We go against our intuition all the time. We see a glass on the edge of a table and we think "Somebody will knock that glass off soon" but do we move it? No. Somebody then knocks the glass off and we say to somebody "I knew that would happen" like we are trying to prove we are of higher intelligence or something. The truth is that our higher intelligence was telling us to move the glass but we ignored it!

Higher intelligence, now there's an idea! Could it be that our intuition is linked to our higher intelligence? Where does that inner feeling come from, you know, the one where something just feels right, or it obviously does not!

The feeling, such as the one when David Beckham lined up to take a free kick for England at Old Trafford against Greece in a world cup qualifier. It was the last kick of the game and it was thirty yards from goal. If he scored we would qualify for the World Cup finals, if not the game would end and we would be unsuccessful. Am I the only Englishman who knew the ball was going to fly into the net and score the goal we needed? I suspect not, but I *KNEW* he was going to score even though I didn't know I was psychic then.

I see intuition being challenged when I am teaching. I see a hand go down to the gear lever then return back quickly to the steering wheel in a change of mind. Intuition has told the driver to change gear but the logical mind has stepped in and cancelled the action, almost as if to say "Hang on, do you know what you are doing?" But intuition had already sent the signal to the hand to do what needed to be done.

This is true in life, especially when it comes to looks and appearance.

The next time you go into a shop and see an item of clothing you are drawn to, then buy it. Obviously check the price first to save embarrassment, but your intuition has drawn you to it. Let me explain.

A pair of red shoes has drawn you to them in a shop and you look at them adoringly. Intuition has decided they are what you need. But the logical mind comes in and starts making you doubt your decision with questions like "Will they go with anything I have at home?", "I will look silly in red shoes at the pub, people only know me for wearing black shoes", "I will need to buy a new wardrobe to go with them and I can't afford that". I know you are all reading this with your heads shamefully in your hands!

This can now go one of two ways.

Option 1

You buy the shoes and wear them to the pub that night. You feel good wearing them and everybody notices and you get lots of good comments like "I love your shoes" if you are a woman or "What's with the red shoes you ladies' man" if you are a man!

Option 2

You ignore the red shoes and opt for a pair of safe black ones but go home still thinking about the red ones. You go to the pub in your black shoes and nobody notices. You still have a feeling of what could have been and your night is just like any other night with your friends.

I am not saying that you should have a pair of red shoes in your wardrobe at all times but your intuition will always give you the correct answer as long as you do not ignore it.

I have found out how intuition works during my training from the spirit world and if I ever question what I am told by spirit they always give me the same response –

"Follow your intuition, you will feel if it is right and if it feels right then just accept it."

Intuition is a feeling your soul gives you when it knows what is right for you. It is your connection with your higher self and ultimately your spiritual source. It will not let you down if you follow it, but do not confuse it with the feeling of greed just because you want something.

ACT

Whenever I ask a pupil "What does act mean?" I am never sure what answer to expect. They are slightly surprised when I tell them it just means,"*get on with it!*" It doesn't mean tear out of a junction or go screaming down the road, that's being impetuous, but it means that having assessed and decided what is the best decision then go ahead and do what you decided otherwise you may lose your opportunity!

Isn't this true in life? Sometimes we spend so long procrastinating that we lose the opportunity we had or we forget what it was we were trying to do in the first place.

It is not to be confused with being impetuous though, we should only act when we have made a good decision. How do we know if we have made a good decision? Our intuition will tell us!

As a group of human beings we spend a lot of time doing things we don't like, wishing we had more time to do the things we really want to. We are employed in jobs that we are not really interested in, looking forward to the day we can retire and do the things we really want to do.

The trouble is that when we retire we are sometimes too old or worn out to do the half marathons we promised ourselves when we were thirty-six! Also, we can't afford to go bumming around the world in a camper van, pensions ain't what they used to be!

But until we retire we have to fill our time at work, earning money to pay the mortgage and to pay for the kids' education and keep up the payments on the dream car we managed to stretch to afford!

Most people never seem to find that dream job - those who do are very lucky and are usually well aware of it.

Deep inside we can feel what makes us tick and what really brings out the passion in us.

I have a friend whose passion is physiotherapy, not necessarily as a science, but he loves the effects it has on the people he treats.

Start a conversation with most people and it won't be too long before they start to tell you about their passion in life. You will recognize it because you will feel the passion as they tell you and you will see it in their eyes and hear it in their voice. There is a local man who is passionate about newts but it is only when he starts to speak about them that you will feel the energy suddenly rise in him and you are captivated by what he says!

We all have this inner energy, we are all passionate about something. Yet we convince ourselves that it is only a dream with excuses like "I would love to do it but I haven't got the time" or "It's not for the likes of me, I am only a factory worker."

But why not?

Most of the time we live our lives in fear, yet when we are challenged we deny it. We are too scared of what people might think, we are too scared of making a fool of ourselves, we are afraid to speak because people will not listen.

Yet inside each one of us is the brightest light just waiting to shine. We cover it up, afraid of anybody seeing it for fear of seeming big headed, but if we want to really feel alive then that light needs to shine, not just for us, but as an example to others who are feeling the same inhibitions.

People thought I was mad for giving up a management job in the motor trade to become a Driving Instructor. I had a Mercedes company car and all the benefits associated but I wasn't really happy. I wanted to teach, I wanted to help normal people, not the ones who lived in a false environment fuelled by their own ego.

I remember thinking that here I was teaching real people who listened to me, paid me then thanked me, whereas I had been used to people trying to intimidate me on a daily basis. I made the break and never regretted it. I knew I was going to make the break, I had planned it over a couple of years and I never doubted for one minute that it wouldn't happen.

We all get the calling to act occasionally and are usually too fearful to take it, as I know from my own past fears.

I fear nothing now.

I have learned that if my intuition tells me it will be ok then it generally will, even if there are obstacles put in the way (that is part of the challenge).

So, if your intuition tells you there is an opportunity to do something you have a passion to do, my advice is

"Stop messing around and get on with it!"

CHAPTER FOUR

WHO
OR WHAT
IS
GOD?

GOD

The word God seems to bring such diverse reactions to the world today.

Before I was eight and Gillian died, I used to think that God was a man with a beard, dressed in sandals and a kaftan who was the boss and ran Heaven. It seemed to fit at the time from the viewpoint of a child but there are many people who have been brought up in the belief that this is not too far from the truth. Organized religion has us believe that we were created in the image of God so therefore God is a man! Oh dear!

When Gillian died I did what most people would do and blamed God for her death and lost my faith and trust in him. The trust and faith in my family never died but I would not re visit my faith in God for forty years or so.

"The love of God is never ending and will not die. The hurt you feel is to prepare you for the road ahead. Do not think that God has forgotten you in your time of need. Wherever you go he will be there with you." Rising Moon.

So who do I think God is now? Well, certainly not who but what. God is not a real person and never has been. The human brain has become three dimensional as our quest for physical and material things has become insatiable. We lost our spiritual contact with God a long time ago and, as a result, the spirit world withdrew their contact with us to a point where they became invisible to the human eye.

We look at ancient cultures with their rituals and love of the earth and see them as inferior to our modern technological world. How arrogant are we? The legend of Atlantis was no legend at all, it was a great and loving society which used powers we can only to dream of, powers that would now be called magic and which people have been persecuted for using. Yet even Atlantis disappeared as its people succumbed to ego and abused their powers for physical wealth. The old saying goes that "You can't take it with you when you die" but we still strive to accumulate as much as we can before we go!

We look at the night sky and believe we are the only race capable of the level of consciousness we currently have. How arrogant are we? The level of consciousness we have on earth at the moment is mainly third dimensional, stuck in the senses of sight, sound, and touch. If we cannot see, hear, or touch it then it cannot possibly exist. Yet there are many levels to consciousness we have not experienced and we may not until after our death, for then we return to spirit and the wonderful feeling of unconditional love. We get excited at the prospect of tiny micro-organisms being found on Mars – possibly. Yet Mars shows all the signs of being a planet just like ours, supported by a higher intelligence. Who is to say that life on Mars was not terminated by the higher intelligence that watches over us?

When we look around the world we see all different kinds of cultures all with their own spiritual foundations. The Native Americans refer to the Great Spirit and they talk of being at one with the land and the animals. Paganism is seen as primitive but they have the same love and respect for the land and the animals. If you scratch the surface of any religion you will see the same connections between land, plants, animals, ourselves and the Universe. We are all one of the same. Man is made of every element found in the Universe and every element of the Universe is found in Man. Understand this and you can understand why we were created in the image of God.

We are all part of something far bigger than we can imagine, remember the bigger picture I keep talking about. It is because of our limited understanding and our need to quantify things that we cannot accept the presence of a higher intelligence. When we open our hearts and accept the possibility of a greater consciousness then the love of that consciousness can come through. If we close the door to it, as we do at present, then we will only see the darkness within the walls we have created. If we open the door to the possibility, then we will start to let in the sunlight that is unconditional love working for our benefit. We do not need to become spiritual or sell our souls to God, we just have to accept the possibility and it will start to work for us.

I try not to use the word "God" simply because it makes me look like a bible basher or born again Christian, and the Christian faith has led many people down the wrong blind alleys over the centuries to protect its own status and power. The words of Jesus have been abused by many organizations, including religions, to keep the people in fear of the consequences of questioning the so called Spiritual leaders. Don't get me wrong, for there have been many inspirational people who have worked in the name of God but also many who have kept their power by instilling a fear of God.

I prefer to call it "the energy" for that is what it is. You can't see it, hear it, touch it, but you can feel it. I have talked about intuition and that is exactly what it is, the feeling that something is right for you or the feeling that something is not right. Throughout this book certain parts will have felt right and some not so right. This is your truth and yours alone so do not try and change it to fit in with society or to please my feelings.

We can and must learn from the animal kingdom. How does a young bird know how to fly? Who teaches it? They might see their parents do it but they certainly don't read a book, watch a DVD, or look it up on the Internet! There are no Bird Flying Instructors that Mummy and Daddy bird can ring up and take their excited youngsters to. So how do they know? Trial and error comes into it but there has to be an inner knowledge of where to start otherwise the young birds would just sit there looking confused!

Prayer is often seen as something that the desperate do but if you only pray when you are desperate you are already in trouble! A prayer is just a thought so let's not get into the realms of reciting a prepared speech set out in a certain way so that God can hear you! A prayer is only a thought, so therefore isn't every thought a prayer? How many times do you hear sportsmen "Thanking God" for their victory and we sometimes cringe at the apparent shallowness of it? We see footballers cross themselves when they come on as a substitute before kicking lumps out of the opposition!

The next time you have a really nice day or even just a nice thought say "Thank you" quietly in your mind and you will be heard. If you suddenly find the solution to a problem you have been worrying about, say "Thank you" just as you would if a close friend had suggested it, because that is what has just happened!

The Spirit world works with us all the time and should not be feared. We have been conditioned by horror films and the scare mongering amongst the media to believe that if it is unbelievable then it is working for the Devil and shouldn't be trusted. But if you ask your friends in the Spirit world and the Angels to protect you while you go about your business they will hear and walk with you.

Crazy I know but try this next time you need some help with a headache or some niggling pain. Ask the Universe and your friends in the Spirit World if they could ease the pain so you can get some comfort then go about your business. Remember that the intention is the important thing and ask as if you mean it! If you suddenly realize later on that your pain is a lot more bearable then is it not possible that your request was heard and acted on? If this was the case then could these same people not help you again? They won't mend broken legs but in my limited experience as a healer I have seen remarkable things happen when healing has been asked for, sometimes involving my own illness and injury.

So if these people are helping us then surely they can be treated as friends. I speak to my people all the time, in fact, when I go to meditate with my spirit guide I tell my wife I am going for a Management Meeting! I treat them as equals and I know they give me unconditional love and do not judge me for what I have done or am doing now or will do. I am on Earth to learn and they will support me through that learning, just like any teacher would. Imagine if a Spirit Guide wouldn't help you because he thought you supported the wrong football team!

So who is God?

God is the energy that every culture on Earth draws from where God is only a name. I think the Native Americans have a better name when they call it the Great Spirit. Call it what you will and do not fear it, treat it as an equal because we are all part of that energy and that energy is part of us all in our intuition.

If you are still not sure I will ask Rising Moon for his final thoughts.

THE THOUGHTS OF RISING MOON

You seek assurance in your daily lives of the things you do and try to achieve yet you already know what you are doing without having to be told. The Great Spirit watches over you and is there to help and work with you. The energy is strong and powerful and should not be ignored, although you do. In your hour of need many questions are asked about the reasons for this episode in your life, but your life would not be complete without this episode. It is with our help and love you can come through these troubled times and become the free spirit you truly are. Every man and every woman has the ability to run free on earth and fulfill the dreams and wishes you have deep in your heart, but let go of the chains that are holding you back. Listen to your heart, listen to your gut instinct, do not be afraid, we will not let you fall.

Breathe in the energy as if it was air, breathe in the love of spirit and release yourselves from the constraints of the physical world. Rise up against your ego. Rise up against your conditioning, question your soul. Find out what it is that you want to do and do it. Do not feel it is for somebody else. You have one life on this earth to live at this moment. Although you may return several times in different forms you will never get this chance again to live the life you are currently living. Go forth and tread your path with a loving and peaceful heart, let the earth benefit from your wisdom while you are here but never let the sound of your voice become too familiar.

I thank you for the chance to communicate with you, the spirit world enjoys your company. Be assured we act only for the good of the soul, your soul journey will not be travelled alone

Go in peace and love

Rising Moon Navajo Chief

THE FINAL CHAPTER

THE FINAL CHAPTER

If you are one of those people who like to read the end of the book to see if the book is worth reading, then this is for you

Follow your intuition!

23815486R00105

Printed in Great Britain
by Amazon